A VOICE FROM THE SOUTH

DOVER THRIFT EDITIONS

Anna Julia Cooper

Introduction by Janet Neary

DOVER PUBLICATIONS, INC.
MINEOLA, NEW YORK

DOVER THRIFT EDITIONS

GENERAL EDITOR: SUSAN L. RATTINER

Bibliographical Note

This Dover edition, first published in 2016, is an unabridged republication of the
work originally published by The Aldine Printing House, Xenia, Ohio, in 1892.
An Introduction written by Janet Neary has been specially prepared for the present
edition.

Library of Congress Cataloging-in-Publication Data

Names: Cooper, Anna J. (Anna Julia), 1858–1964, author.
Title: A voice from the south / Anna Julia Cooper ; introduction by Janet Neary.
Description: Mineola, New York: Dover Publications, Inc., 2016. | Series: Dover
    thrift editions
Identifiers: LCCN 2016002408 | ISBN 9780486805634 | ISBN 0486805638
Subjects: LCSH: African American women—Southern States—Social
    Conditions—19th century. | African American women—Southern States—
    History—19th century. | African Americans—Southern States—Social
    conditions—19th century. | African Americans—Southern States—History—
    19th century. | Southern States—Race relations.
Classification: LCC E185.86 .C587 2016 | DDC 305.48/896073075—dc23
LC record available at http://lccn.loc.gov/2016002408

Manufactured in the United States by LSC Communications
80563807   2020
www.doverpublications.com

INTRODUCTION

An Arc of Light:
Anna Julia Cooper's *A Voice from the South*

WRITTEN IN 1892, Anna Julia Cooper's groundbreaking essay collection *A Voice from the South, by A Black Woman of the South* is a cornerstone of black feminist and political theory, a literary achievement, and a call to action that remains relevant today. As an interrogation of power, a critique of empiricism, and a revelatory work of intersectional analysis, Cooper's contribution in *Voice* is often condensed into her now well-known declaration, "Only the Black Woman can say, 'when and where I enter, in the quiet undisputed dignity of my womanhood, without violence and without suing or special patronage, then and there the whole *Negro race enters with me.*'"[1] However, as one scholar has observed, the relatively recent prominence the text enjoys "belies the arduous history that characterized Cooper's attempts to secure a public voice in print" during her own life.[2] This edition of her book owes its existence to black feminist scholars' recovery and reclamation efforts that began in the 1970s and must be viewed in light of the genealogy of black women's intellectual, literary, political, and social history which is only now receiving more widespread scholarly attention.[3]

Born into slavery in Raleigh, North Carolina, in 1858, Cooper rose to prominence as a leading scholar, educator, and activist at the end of the nineteenth century, producing *Voice* while she was the principal of the renowned M Street High School in Washington, D.C. An active public intellectual, Cooper was selected to speak before the World's Congress of Representative Women in 1893 and at the Pan-African Congress Conference in London in 1900.[4] In 1925, she became the fourth African American woman to receive her doctorate, which she did at the age of sixty-six, from the Paris-Sorbonne University. In the midst of her robust scholarly career, at the age of fifty-seven, Cooper adopted five orphaned children under the age of thirteen.[5] Although *Voice* was her only full-length book, her writing and scholarship continued to evolve over the course of her long life (she lived to be 105), most notably in her doctoral dissertation, *Slavery and the French Revolutionists, 1788–1805*, as well as in the variety of her essays, speeches, letters, and memoirs.[6] As both her life history and doctoral research show, Cooper was "a key theorist in the emergence of new forms of black internationalism"; nevertheless, her work is often overlooked in favor of more celebrated black men, such as W. E. B. DuBois and C. L. R. James, for whom she was an important and often unacknowledged interlocutor.[7]

Characterized by an emphasis on debate and her inimitable wit, the essays which comprise *Voice* feel simultaneously urgent and modern even while they bear the imprint of late-nineteenth-century social thought. In a passage which showcases both her rhetorical savvy and her analysis of the ways power dictates the very terms of social definition, Cooper rejects external determinations of what is considered "womanly," arguing that the world needs more "women who can think as well as feel, and who feel none the less because they think."[8] Because of passages like this, Cooper has been criticized for hewing to the limited, ideologically freighted conventions of "True Womanhood"; however, the question remains open whether or not her assessment of women's leadership as more "sympathetic" than men's is an example of her taking up a dissident position within available narrative forms. In this vein, Vivian May—the author of the most comprehensive study of Cooper's work to date—argues that *Voice* constitutes "a contestatory form of speaking up that both shatters and departs from dominant discourse."[9]

Cooper's polemical style and insistence on embodied knowledge are also key to *Voice*'s value as a work of literary criticism. At a moment when black authors were subject to patronizing protocols authorizing their literary contributions, Cooper defiantly takes up the position of the critic, piercing the assumption that white authors have access to universal truth. She criticizes William Dean Howells, among others, for tone-deaf and spurious characterizations of black people, which they offered as representative. Yet Cooper's polemicism and close engagement with the social logic of her time are also responsible for the most troubling aspects of the text: its orientalism and Islamophobia. Overturning received notions of environmental determinism, Cooper underscores the vitality of black people—highlighting both their cultural accomplishments and biological potential—in part by drawing on racial hierarchies inherent in now outdated notions of "civilization."[10]

Cooper's intersectional analysis and insistence on black women's essential role in social progress remain central to a contemporary scholarly agenda, even while her engagement with the social preoccupations and literary forms of her time mark its limits.[11] Perhaps, in the final assessment, we would do well to hew close to Cooper's own words: "No finite mind can grasp and give out the whole circle of truth. We do well if we can illuminate just the tiny arc which we occupy and should be glad that the next generation will not need the lessons we try so assiduously to hammer into this."[12]

JANET NEARY

Notes

1 Anna Julia Cooper, *A Voice from the South* (New York: Oxford University Press, 1988): 31.

2 Shirley Moody-Turner, "'Dear Doctor Du Bois': Anna Julia Cooper, W. E. B. Du Bois, and the Gender Politics of Black Publishing," *MELUS* 40.3 (Fall 2015): 47-68, 47.

3 Cooper belongs to a formidable group of black women scholars and activists in the late nineteenth century, including Maria Stewart, Sojourner Truth, Fannie Barrier Williams, Charlotte Forten Grimké, Ida B. Wells, Fannie Jackson Coppin, Victoria Earle Matthews, Frances Harper, and Mary Church Terrell. The following texts place Cooper's legacy in the context of these other black women scholars and activists: Mary Helen Washington, Introduction, *A Voice from the South* (New York: Oxford University Press, 1988): li; Vivian M. May, "Writing the Self into Being: Anna Julia Cooper's Textual Politics," *African American Review* 43.1 (Spring 2009): 17-34, 17; and Beverly Guy-Sheftall, "Black Feminist Studies: The Case of Anna Julia Cooper," *African American Review* 43.1 (Spring 2009): 11-15, 11.

4 For a more comprehensive biography, see Mary Helen Washington, Introduction, *A Voice from the South* (New York: Oxford University Press, 1988).

5 As Washington notes, the children "ranged in age from six months to twelve years and were the grandchildren of her half-brother," xxxviii.

6 Anna Julia Cooper, *Slavery and the French Revolutionists, 1788-1805.* Trans. Frances Richardson Keller (Lewiston, NY: Edwin Mellen Press, 1988). On her other writings, see *The Voice of Anna Julia Cooper: Including a Voice*

from the South and Other Important Essays, Papers, and Letters, Eds. Charles Lemert and Esme Bhan (New York: Rowman & Littlefield Publishers, 1998): 306. Lemert and Bhan's book reprints much of her writing, including her two memoirs—one reflecting on her experiences at the Sorbonne and the other offering reminiscences of the Grimké family and her early years in D.C. On the evolution of Cooper's writing, Moody-Turner writes that "By adding an examination of the material and political consequences of popular portrayals of African Americans and by critiquing her earlier position on voice, voicelessness, power, and domination, [Cooper's] later texts suggest that [she]…continued to reflect on and revise her critical strategies for promoting agency, voice, and self-definition," 8.

7 Shirley Moody-Turner, Preface, "Anna Julia Cooper: A Voice beyond the South," *African American Review* 43.1 (Spring 2009): 7-9, 7.

8 Cooper, 50.

9 May, "Writing," 17.

10 See Kyla Schuller, *Biopolitics of Feeling: Race, Sex, and Impressibility in the Nineteenth-Century United States* (forthcoming from Duke University Press).

11 Cooper's influence is evidenced by the intellectual debt acknowledged by the most foundational black feminist texts of our own era, including Paula Giddings' *When and Where I Enter: The Impact of Black Women on Race and Sex in America* (1984) and Hazel Carby's *Reconstructing Womanhood: The Emergence of the Afro-American Woman Novelist* (1987), both of which quote *A Voice from the South* in their titles—Giddings' book title and Carby's chapter "'In the Quiet, Undisputed Dignity of My Womanhood': Black Feminist Thought after Emancipation."

12 Cooper, 183.

A VOICE FROM THE SOUTH

"WITH REGRET
I FORGET
IF THE SONG BE LIVING YET,
   YET REMEMBER, VAGUELY NOW,
   IT <u>WAS</u> <u>HONEST,</u> <u>ANYHOW.</u>"

TO
Bishop Benjamin William Arnett,

WITH PROFOUND REGARD FOR HIS HEROIC DEVOTION TO

GOD AND THE RACE,

both in Church and in State,—and with sincere esteem for his unselfish espousal of the cause of the Black Woman and of every human interest that lacks a Voice and needs a Defender, this, the primary utterance of my heart and pen,

IS AFFECTIONATELY INSCRIBED.

Contents

PART FIRST

Soprano Obligato

PART SECOND

Tutti ad Libitum

SOPRANO OBLIGATO

For they the *Royal-hearted Women* are
Who nobly love the noblest, yet have grace
For needy, suffering lives in lowliest place;
Carrying a choicer sunlight in their smile,
The heavenliest ray that pitieth the vile.

★ ★ ★

Though I were happy, throned beside the king,
I should be tender to each little thing
With hurt warm breast, that had no speech to tell
Its inward pangs; and I would sooth it well
With tender touch and with a low, soft moan
For company.

—*George Eliot.*

OUR RAISON D'ÊTRE

IN THE CLASH and clatter of our American Conflict, it has been said that the South remains Silent. Like the Sphinx she inspires vociferous disputation, but herself takes little part in the noisy controversy. One muffled strain in the Silent South, a jarring chord and a vague and uncomprehended cadenza has been and still is the Negro. And of that muffled chord, the one mute and voiceless note has been the sadly expectant Black Woman,

> An infant crying in the night,
> An infant crying for the light;
> And with *no language—but a cry*.

The colored man's inheritance and apportionment is still the sombre crux, the perplexing *cul de sac* of the nation,—the dumb skeleton in the closet provoking ceaseless harangues, indeed, but little understood and seldom consulted. Attorneys for the plaintiff and attorneys for the defendant, with bungling *gaucherie* have analyzed and dissected, theorized and synthesized with sublime ignorance or pathetic misapprehension of counsel from the black client. One important witness has not yet been heard from. The summing up of the evidence deposed, and the charge to the jury have been made—but no word from the Black Woman.

It is because I believe the American people to be conscientiously committed to a fair trial and ungarbled evidence, and because I feel it essential to a perfect understanding and an equitable verdict that truth from *each* standpoint be presented at the bar,—that this little Voice has been added to the already full chorus. The "other side" has not been represented by one who "lives there." And not many can more sensibly realize and more accurately tell the weight and the fret of the "long dull pain" than the open-eyed but hitherto voiceless Black Woman of America.

The feverish agitation, the perfervid energy, the busy objectivity of the more turbulent life of our men serves, it may be, at once to cloud or color their vision somewhat, and as well to relieve the smart and deaden the pain for them. Their voice is in consequence not always temperate and calm, and at the same time radically corrective and sanatory. At any rate, as our Caucasian barristers are not to blame if they cannot *quite* put themselves in the dark man's place, neither should the dark man be wholly expected fully and adequately to reproduce the exact Voice of the Black Woman.

Delicately sensitive at every pore to social atmospheric conditions, her calorimeter may well be studied in the interest of accuracy and fairness in diagnosing what is often conceded to be a "puzzling" case. If these broken utterances can in any way help to a clearer vision and a truer pulse-beat in studying our Nation's Problem, this Voice by a Black Woman of the South will not have been raised in vain.

Tawawa Chimney Corner;
   Sept. 17, 1892.

★WOMANHOOD A VITAL ELEMENT
IN THE REGENERATION AND
PROGRESS OF A RACE

THE TWO SOURCES from which, perhaps, modern civilization has derived its noble and ennobling ideal of woman are Christianity and the Feudal System.

In Oriental countries woman has been uniformly devoted to a life of ignorance, infamy, and complete stagnation. The Chinese shoe of to-day does not more entirely dwarf, cramp, and destroy her physical powers, than have the customs, laws, and social instincts, which from remotest ages have governed our Sister of the East, enervated and blighted her mental and moral life.

Mahomet makes no account of woman whatever in his polity. The Koran, which, unlike our Bible, was a product and not a growth, tried to address itself to the needs of Arabian civilization as Mahomet with his circumscribed powers saw them. The Arab was a nomad. Home to him meant his present camping place. That deity who, according to our western ideals, makes and sanctifies the home, was to him a transient bauble to be toyed with so long as it gave pleasure and then to be thrown aside for a new one. As a personality, an individual soul, capable of eternal growth and unlimited development, and destined to mould and shape the civilization of the future to an incalculable extent, Mahomet did not know woman. There was no hereafter, no paradise for her. The heaven of the Mussulman is peopled and made gladsome not by the departed wife, or sister, or mother, but by *houri*—a figment of Mahomet's brain, partaking of the ethereal qualities of angels, yet imbued with all the vices and inanity of Oriental women. The harem here, and—"dust to dust"

---

* Read before the convocation of colored clergy of the Protestant Episcopal Church at Washington, D. C., 1886.

1

hereafter, this was the hope, the inspiration, the *summum bonum* of the Eastern woman's life! With what result on the life of the nation, the "Unspeakable Turk," the "sick man" of modern Europe can to-day exemplify.

Says a certain writer: "The private life of the Turk is vilest of the vile, unprogressive, unambitious, and inconceivably low." And yet Turkey is not without her great men. She has produced most brilliant minds; men skilled in all the intricacies of diplomacy and statesmanship; men whose intellects could grapple with the deep problems of empire and manipulate the subtle agencies which check-mate kings. But these minds were not the normal outgrowth of a healthy trunk. They seemed rather ephemeral excrescencies which shoot far out with all the vigor and promise, apparently, of strong branches; but soon alas fall into decay and ugliness because there is no soundness in the root, no life-giving sap, permeating, strengthening and perpetuating the whole. There is a worm at the core! The homelife is impure! and when we look for fruit, like apples of Sodom, it crumbles within our grasp into dust and ashes.

It is pleasing to turn from this effete and immobile civilization to a society still fresh and vigorous, whose seed is in itself, and whose very name is synonymous with all that is progressive, elevating and inspiring, viz., the European bud and the American flower of modern civilization.

And here let me say parenthetically that our satisfaction in American institutions rests not on the fruition we now enjoy, but springs rather from the possibilities and promise that are inherent in the system, though as yet, perhaps, far in the future.

"Happiness," says Madame de Stael, "consists not in perfections attained, but in a sense of progress, the result of our own endeavor under conspiring circumstances *toward* a goal which continually advances and broadens and deepens till it is swallowed up in the Infinite." Such conditions in embryo are all that we claim for the land of the West. We have not yet reached our ideal in American civilization. The pessimists even declare that we are not marching in that direction. But there can be no doubt that here in America is the arena in which the next triumph of civilization is to be won; and here too we find promise abundant and possibilities infinite.

Now let us see on what basis this hope for our country primarily and fundamentally rests. Can any one doubt that it is chiefly on the homelife and on the influence of good women in those homes? Says

Macaulay: "You may judge a nation's rank in the scale of civilization from the way they treat their women." And Emerson, "I have thought that a sufficient measure of civilization is the influence of good women." Now this high regard for woman, this germ of a prolific idea which in our own day is bearing such rich and varied fruit, was ingrafted into European civilization, we have said, from two sources, the Christian Church and the Feudal System. For although the Feudal System can in no sense be said to have originated the idea, yet there can be no doubt that the habits of life and modes of thought to which Feudalism gave rise, materially fostered and developed it; for they gave us chivalry, than which no institution has more sensibly magnified and elevated woman's position in society.

Tacitus dwells on the tender regard for woman entertained by these rugged barbarians before they left their northern homes to overrun Europe. Old Norse legends too, and primitive poems, all breathe the same spirit of love of home and veneration for the pure and noble influence there presiding—the wife, the sister, the mother.

And when later on we see the settled life of the Middle Ages "oozing out," as M. Guizot expresses it, from the plundering and pillaging life of barbarism and crystallizing into the Feudal System, the tiger of the field is brought once more within the charmed circle of the goddesses of his castle, and his imagination weaves around them a halo whose reflection possibly has not yet altogether vanished.

It is true the spirit of Christianity had not yet put the seal of catholicity on this sentiment. Chivalry, according to Bascom, was but the toning down and softening of a rough and lawless period. It gave a roseate glow to a bitter winter's day. Those who looked out from castle windows revelled in its "amethyst tints." But God's poor, the weak, the unlovely, the commonplace were still freezing and starving none the less in unpitied, unrelieved loneliness.

Respect for woman, the much lauded chivalry of the Middle Ages, meant what I fear it still means to some men in our own day— respect for the elect few among whom they expect to consort.

The idea of the radical amelioration of womankind, reverence for woman as woman regardless of rank, wealth, or culture, was to come from that rich and bounteous fountain from which flow all our liberal and universal ideas—the Gospel of Jesus Christ.

And yet the Christian Church at the time of which we have been speaking would seem to have been doing even less to protect and elevate woman than the little done by secular society. The Church as an organization committed a double offense against woman in the Middle Ages. Making of marriage a sacrament and at the same time insisting on the celibacy of the clergy and other religious orders, she gave an inferior if not an impure character to the marriage relation, especially fitted to reflect discredit on woman. Would this were all or the worst! but the Church by the licentiousness of its chosen servants invaded the household and established too often as vicious connections those relations which it forbade to assume openly and in good faith. "Thus," to use the words of our authority, "the religious corps became as numerous, as searching, and as unclean as the frogs of Egypt, which penetrated into all quarters, into the ovens and kneading troughs, leaving their filthy trail wherever they went." Says Chaucer with characteristic satire, speaking of the Friars:

> 'Women may now go safely up and doun,
> In every bush, and under every tree,
> Ther is non other incubus but he,
> And he ne will don hem no dishonour.'

Henry, Bishop of Liege, could unblushingly boast the birth of twenty-two children in fourteen years.[*]

It may help us under some of the perplexities which beset our way in "the one Catholic and Apostolic Church" to-day, to recall some of the corruptions and incongruities against which the Bride of Christ has had to struggle in her past history and in spite of which she has kept, through many vicissitudes, the faith once delivered to the saints. Individuals, organizations, whole sections of the Church militant may outrage the Christ whom they profess, may ruthlessly trample under foot both the spirit and the letter of his precepts, yet not till we hear the voices audibly saying "Come let us depart hence," shall we cease to believe and cling to the promise, "*I am with you to the end of the world.*"

> "Yet saints their watch are keeping,
> The cry goes up 'How long!'
> And soon the night of weeping
> Shall be the morn of song."

---

[*] Bascom.

However much then the facts of any particular period of history may seem to deny it, I for one do not doubt that the source of the vitalizing principle of woman's development and amelioration is the Christian Church, so far as that church is coincident with Christianity.

Christ gave ideals not formulæ. The Gospel is a germ requiring millennia for its growth and ripening. It needs and at the same time helps to form around itself a soil enriched in civilization, and perfected in culture and insight without which the embryo can neither be unfolded or comprehended. With all the strides our civilization has made from the first to the nineteenth century, we can boast not an idea, not a principle of action, not a progressive social force but was already mutely foreshadowed, or directly enjoined in that simple tale of a meek and lowly life. The quiet face of the Nazarene is ever seen a little way ahead, never too far to come down to and touch the life of the lowest in days the darkest, yet ever leading onward, still onward, the tottering childish feet of our strangely boastful civilization.

By laying down for woman the same code of morality, the same standard of purity, as for man; by refusing to countenance the shameless and equally guilty monsters who were gloating over her fall,—graciously stooping in all the majesty of his own spotlessness to wipe away the filth and grime of her guilty past and bid her go in peace and sin no more; and again in the moments of his own careworn and footsore dejection, turning trustfully and lovingly, away from the heartless snubbing and sneers, away from the cruel malignity of mobs and prelates in the dusty marts of Jerusalem to the ready sympathy, loving appreciation and unfaltering friendship of that quiet home at Bethany; and even at the last, by his dying bequest to the disciple whom he loved, signifying the protection and tender regard to be extended to that sorrowing mother and ever afterward to the sex she represented;—throughout his life and in his death he has given to men a rule and guide for the estimation of woman as an equal, as a helper, as a friend, and as a sacred charge to be sheltered and cared for with a brother's love and sympathy, lessons which nineteen centuries' gigantic strides in knowledge, arts, and sciences, in social and ethical principles have not been able to probe to their depth or to exhaust in practice.

It seems not too much to say then of the vitalizing, regenerating, and progressive influence of womanhood on the civilization of today, that, while it was foreshadowed among Germanic nations in the far away dawn of their history as a narrow, sickly and stunted growth, it yet owes its catholicity and power, the deepening of its roots and broadening of its branches to Christianity.

The union of these two forces, the Barbaric and the Christian, was not long delayed after the Fall of the Empire. The Church, which fell with Rome, finding herself in danger of being swallowed up by barbarism, with characteristic vigor and fertility of resources, addressed herself immediately to the task of conquering her conquerers. The means chosen does credit to her power of penetration and adaptability, as well as to her profound, unerring, all-compassing diplomacy; and makes us even now wonder if aught human can successfully and ultimately withstand her far-seeing designs and brilliant policy, or gainsay her well-earned claim to the word *Catholic*.

She saw the barbarian, little more developed than a wild beast. She forbore to antagonize and mystify his warlike nature by a full blaze of the heartsearching and humanizing tenets of her great Head. She said little of the rule "If thy brother smite thee on one cheek, turn to him the other also;" but thought it sufficient for the needs of those times, to establish the so-called "Truce of God" under which men were bound to abstain from butchering one another for three days of each week and on Church festivals. In other words, she respected their individuality: non-resistance pure and simple being for them an utter impossibility, she contented herself with less radical measures calculated to lead up finally to the full measure of the benevolence of Christ.

Next she took advantage of the barbarian's sensuous love of gaudy display and put all her magnificent garments on. She could not capture him by physical force, she would dazzle him by gorgeous spectacles. It is said that Romanism gained more in pomp and ritual during this trying period of the Dark Ages than throughout all her former history.

The result was she carried her point. Once more Rome laid her ambitious hand on the temporal power, and allied with Charlemagne, aspired to rule the world through a civilization dominated by Christianity and permeated by the traditions and instincts of those sturdy barbarians.

Here was the confluence of the two streams we have been tracing, which, united now, stretch before us as a broad majestic river.

In regard to woman it was the meeting of two noble and ennobling forces, two kindred ideas the resultant of which, we doubt not, is destined to be a potent force in the betterment of the world.

Now after our appeal to history comparing nations destitute of this force and so destitute also of the principle of progress, with other nations among whom the influence of woman is prominent coupled with a brisk, progressive, satisfying civilization,—if in addition we find this strong presumptive evidence corroborated by reason and experience, we may conclude that these two equally varying concomitants are linked as cause and effect; in other words, that the position of woman in society determines the vital elements of its regeneration and progress.

Now that this is so on *a priori* grounds all must admit. And this not because woman is better or stronger or wiser than man, but from the nature of the case, because it is she who must first form the man by directing the earliest impulses of his character.

Byron and Wordsworth were both geniuses and would have stamped themselves on the thought of their age under any circumstances; and yet we find the one a savor of life unto life, the other of death unto death. "Byron, like a rocket, shot his way upward with scorn and repulsion, flamed out in wild, explosive, brilliant excesses and disappeared in darkness made all the more palpable."[*]

Wordsworth lent of his gifts to reinforce that "power in the Universe which makes for righteousness" by taking the harp handed him from Heaven and using it to swell the strains of angelic choirs. Two locomotives equally mighty stand facing opposite tracks; the one to rush headlong to destruction with all its precious freight, the other to toil grandly and gloriously up the steep embattlements to Heaven and to God. Who—who can say what a world of consequences hung on the first placing and starting of these enormous forces!

Woman, Mother,—your responsibility is one that might make angels tremble and fear to take hold! To trifle with it, to ignore or misuse it, is to treat lightly the most sacred and solemn trust ever confided by God to human kind. The training of children is a task on which an infinity of weal or woe depends. Who does not covet it? Yet who does not stand awe-struck before its momentous issues!

---

[*] Bascom's Eng. Lit, p. 253.

It is a matter of small moment, it seems to me, whether that lovely girl in whose accomplishments you take such pride and delight, can enter the gay and crowded salon with the ease and elegance of this or that French or English gentlewoman, compared with the decision as to whether her individuality is going to reinforce the good or the evil elements of the world. The lace and the diamonds, the dance and the theater, gain a new significance when scanned in their hearings on such issues. Their influence on the individual personality, and through her on the society and civilization which she vitalizes and inspires—all this and more must be weighed in the balance before the jury can return a just and intelligent verdict as to the innocence or banefulness of these apparently simple amusements.

Now the fact of woman's influence on society being granted, what are its practical bearings on the work which brought together this conference of colored clergy and laymen in Washington? "We come not here to talk." Life is too busy, too pregnant with meaning and far reaching consequences to allow you to come this far for mere intellectual entertainment.

The vital agency of womanhood in the regeneration and progress of a race, as a general question, is conceded almost before it is fairly stated. I confess one of the difficulties for me in the subject assigned lay in its obviousness. The plea is taken away by the opposite attorney's granting the whole question.

"Woman's influence on social progress"—who in Christendom doubts or questions it? One may as well be called on to prove that the sun is the source of light and heat and energy to this many-sided little world.

Nor, on the other hand, could it have been intended that I should apply the position when taken and proven, to the needs and responsibilities of the women of our race in the South. For is it not written, "Cursed is he that cometh after the king?" and has not the King already preceded me in "The Black Woman of the South"?*

They have had both Moses and the Prophets in Dr. Crummell and if they hear not him, neither would they be persuaded though one came up from the South.

I would beg, however, with the Doctor's permission, to add my plea for the *Colored Girls* of the South:—that large, bright, promising

---

* Pamphlet published by Dr. Alex. Crummell.

fatally beautiful class that stand shivering like a delicate plantlet before the fury of tempestuous elements, so full of promise and possibilities, yet so sure of destruction; often without a father to whom they dare apply the loving term, often without a stronger brother to espouse their cause and defend their honor with his life's blood; in the midst of pitfalls and snares, waylaid by the lower classes of white men, with no shelter, no protection nearer than the great blue vault above, which half conceals and half reveals the one Care-Taker they know so little of. Oh, save them, help them, shield, train, develop, teach, inspire them! Snatch them, in God's name, as brands from the burning! There is material in them well worth your while, the hope in germ of a staunch, helpful, regenerating womanhood on which, primarily, rests the foundation stones of our future as a race.

It is absurd to quote statistics showing the Negro's bank account and rent rolls, to point to the hundreds of newspapers edited by colored men and lists of lawyers, doctors, professors, D. D's, LL D's, etc., etc., etc., while the source from which the life-blood of the race is to flow is subject to taint and corruption in the enemy's camp.

True progress is never made by spasms. Real progress is growth. It must begin in the seed. Then, "first the blade, then the ear, after that the full corn in the ear." There is something to encourage and inspire us in the advancement of individuals since their emancipation from slavery. It at least proves that there is nothing irretrievably wrong in the shape of the black man's skull, and that under given circumstances his development, downward or upward, will be similar to that of other average human beings.

But there is no time to be wasted in mere felicitation. That the Negro has his niche in the infinite purposes of the Eternal, no one who has studied the history of the last fifty years in America will deny. That much depends on his own right comprehension of his responsibility and rising to the demands of the hour, it will be good for him to see; and how best to use his present so that the structure of the future shall be stronger and higher and brighter and nobler and holier than that of the past, is a question to be decided each day by every one of us.

The race is just twenty-one years removed from the conception and experience of a chattel, just at the age of ruddy manhood. It is well enough to pause a moment for retrospection, introspection, and prospection. We look back, not to become inflated with conceit because of the depths from which we have arisen, but that we may learn wisdom from experience. We look within that we may gather together once more our forces, and, by improved and more practical methods, address ourselves to the tasks before us. We look forward with hope and trust that the same God whose guiding hand led our fathers through and out of the gall and bitterness of oppression, will still lead and direct their children, to the honor of His name, and for their ultimate salvation.

But this survey of the failures or achievments of the past, the difficulties and embarrassments of the present, and the mingled hopes and fears for the future, must not degenerate into mere dreaming nor consume the time which belongs to the practical and effective handling of the crucial questions of the hour; and there can be no issue more vital and momentous than this of the womanhood of the race.

Here is the vulnerable point, not in the heel, but at the heart of the young Achilles; and here must the defenses be strengthened and the watch redoubled.

We are the heirs of a past which was not our fathers' moulding. "Every man the arbiter of his own destiny" was not true for the American Negro of the past: and it is no fault of his that he finds himself to-day the inheritor of a manhood and womanhood impoverished and debased by two centuries and more of compression and degradation.

But weaknesses and malformations, which to-day are attributable to a vicious schoolmaster and a pernicious system, will a century hence be rightly regarded as proofs of innate corruptness and radical incurability.

Now the fundamental agency under God in the regeneration, the re-training of the race, as well as the ground work and starting point of its progress upward, must be the *black woman*.

With all the wrongs and neglects of her past, with all the weakness, the debasement, the moral thralldom of her present, the black woman of to-day stands mute and wondering at the Herculean task devolving upon her. But the cycles wait for her. No other hand can move the lever. She must be loosed from her bands and set to work.

Our meager and superficial results from past efforts prove their futility; and every attempt to elevate the Negro, whether undertaken by himself or through the philanthropy of others, cannot but prove abortive unless so directed as to utilize the indispensable agency of an elevated and trained womanhood.

A race cannot be purified from without. Preachers and teachers are helps, and stimulants and conditions as necessary as the gracious rain and sunshine are to plant growth. But what are rain and dew and sunshine and cloud if there be no life in the plant germ? We must go to the root and see that that is sound and healthy and vigorous; and not deceive ourselves with waxen flowers and painted leaves of mock chlorophyll.

We too often mistake individuals' honor for race development and so are ready to substitute pretty accomplishments for sound sense and earnest purpose.

A stream cannot rise higher than its source. The atmosphere of homes is no rarer and purer and sweeter than are the mothers in those homes. A race is but a total of families. The nation is the aggregate of its homes. As the whole is sum of all its parts, so the character of the parts will determine the characteristics of the whole. These are all axioms and so evident that it seems gratuitous to remark it; and yet, unless I am greatly mistaken, most of the unsatisfaction from our past results arises from just such a radical and palpable error, as much almost on our own part as on that of our benevolent white friends.

The Negro is constitutionally hopeful and proverbially irrepressible; and naturally stands in danger of being dazzled by the shimmer and tinsel of superficials. We often mistake foliage for fruit and overestimate or wrongly estimate brilliant results.

The late Martin R. Delany, who was an unadulterated black man, used to say when honors of state fell upon him, that when he entered the council of kings the black race entered with him; meaning, I suppose, that there was no discounting his race identity and attributing his achievements to some admixture of Saxon blood. But our present record of eminent men, when placed beside the actual status of the race in America to-day, proves that no man can represent the race. Whatever the attainments of the individual may be, unless his home has moved on *pari passu*, he can never be regarded as identical with or representative of the whole.

Not by pointing to sun-bathed mountain tops do we prove that Phœbus warms the valleys. We must point to homes, average homes, homes of the rank and file of horny handed toiling men and women of the South (where the masses are) lighted and cheered by

the good, the beautiful, and the true,—then and not till then will
the whole plateau be lifted into the sunlight.

Only the BLACK WOMAN can say "when and where I enter, in
the quiet, undisputed dignity of my womanhood, without violence
and without suing or special patronage, then and there the whole
Negro race enters with me." Is it not evident then that as individual
workers for this race we must address ourselves with no half-hearted
zeal to this feature of our mission. The need is felt and must be recognized by all. There is a call for workers, for missionaries, for men
and women with the double consecration of a fundamental love of
humanity and a desire for its melioration through the Gospel; but
superadded to this we demand an intelligent and sympathetic comprehension of the interests and special needs of the Negro.

I see not why there should not be an organized effort for the
protection and elevation of our girls such as the White Cross
League in England. English women are strengthened and protected
by more than twelve centuries of Christian influences, freedom and
civilization; English girls are dispirited and crushed down by no
such all-levelling prejudice as that supercilious caste spirit in
America which cynically assumes "A Negro woman cannot be a
lady." English womanhood is beset by no such snares and traps as
betray the unprotected, untrained colored girl of the South, whose
only crime and dire destruction often is her unconscious and marvelous beauty. Surely then if English indignation is aroused and
English manhood thrilled under the leadership of a Bishop of the
English church to build up bulwarks around their wronged sisters,
Negro sentiment cannot remain callous and Negro effort nerveless
in view of the imminent peril of the mothers of the next generation. "*I am my Sister's keeper!*" should be the hearty response of
every man and woman of the race, and this conviction should
purify and exalt the narrow, selfish and petty personal aims of life
into a noble and sacred purpose.

We need men who can let their interest and gallantry extend
outside the circle of their æsthetic appreciation; men who can be a
father, a brother, a friend to every weak, struggling unshielded girl.
We need women who are so sure of their own social footing that
they need not fear leaning to lend a hand to a fallen or falling sister.
We need men and women who do not exhaust their genius split-
ting hairs on aristocratic distinctions and thanking God they are not
as others; but earnest, unselfish souls, who can go into the highways

and byways, lifting up and leading, advising and encouraging with the truly catholic benevolence of the Gospel of Christ.

As Church workers we must confess our path of duty is less obvious; or rather our ability to adapt our machinery to our conception of the peculiar exigencies of this work as taught by experience and our own consciousness of the needs of the Negro, is as yet not demonstrable. Flexibility and aggressiveness are not such strong characteristics of the Church to-day as in the Dark Ages.

As a Mission field for the Church the Southern Negro is in some aspects most promising; in others, perplexing. Aliens neither in language and customs, nor in associations and sympathies, naturally of deeply rooted religious instincts and taking most readily and kindly to the worship and teachings of the Church, surely the task of proselytizing the American Negro is infinitely less formidable than that which confronted the Church in the Barbarians of Europe. Besides, this people already look to the Church as the hope of their race. Thinking colored men almost uniformly admit that the Protestant Episcopal Church with its quiet, chaste dignity and decorous solemnity, its instructive and elevating ritual, its bright chanting and joyous hymning, is eminently fitted to correct the peculiar faults of worship—the rank exuberance and often ludicrous demonstrativeness of their people. Yet, strange to say, the Church, claiming to be missionary and Catholic, urging that schism is sin and denominationalism inexcusable, has made in all these years almost no inroads upon this semi-civilized religionism.

Harvests from this over ripe field of home missions have been gathered in by Methodists, Baptists, and not least by Congregationalists, who were unknown to the Freedmen before their emancipation.

Our clergy numbers less than two dozen* priests of Negro blood and we have hardly more than one self-supporting colored congregation in the entire Southland. While the organization known as the A. M. E. Church has 14,063 ministers, itinerant and local, 4,069 self-supporting churches, 4,275 Sunday-schools, with property valued at $7,772,284, raising yearly for church purposes $1,427,000.

---

* The published report of '91 shows 26 priests for the entire country, including one not engaged in work and one a professor in a non-sectarian school, since made Dean of an Episcopal Annex to Howard University known as King Hall.

Stranger and more significant than all, the leading men of this race (I do not mean demagogues and politicians, but men of intellect, heart, and race devotion, men to whom the elevation of their people means more than personal ambition and sordid gain—and the men of that stamp have not all died yet) the Christian workers for the race, of younger and more cultured growth, are noticeably drifting into sectarian churches, many of them declaring all the time that they acknowledge the historic claims of the Church, believe her apostolicity, and would experience greater personal comfort, spiritual and intellectual, in her revered communion. It is a fact which any one may verify for himself, that representative colored men, professing that in their heart of hearts they are Episcopalians, are actually working in Methodist and Baptist pulpits; while the ranks of the Episcopal clergy are left to be filled largely by men who certainly suggest the propriety of a *"perpetual* Diaconate" if they cannot be said to have created the necessity for it.

Now where is the trouble? Something must be wrong. What is it?

A certain Southern Bishop of our Church reviewing the situation, whether in Godly anxiety or in "Gothic antipathy" I know not, deprecates the fact that the colored people do not seem *drawn* to the Episcopal Church, and comes to the sage conclusion that the Church is not adapted to the rude untutored minds of the Freedmen, and that they may be left to go to the Methodists and Baptists whither their racial proclivities undeniably tend. How the good Bishop can agree that all-foreseeing Wisdom, and Catholic Love would have framed his Church as typified in his seamless garment and unbroken body, and yet not leave it broad enough and deep enough and loving enough to seek and save and hold seven millions of God's poor, I cannot see.

But the doctors while discussing their scientifically conclusive diagnosis of the disease, will perhaps not think it presumptuous in the patient if he dares to suggest where at least the pain is. If this be allowed, a *Black woman of the South* would beg to point out two possible oversights in this southern work which may indicate in part both a cause and a remedy for some failure. The first is *not calculating for the Black man's personality;* not having respect, if I may so express it, to his manhood or deferring at all to his conceptions of the needs of his people. When colored persons have been employed it was too often as machines or as manikins. There has been no disposition, generally, to get the black man's ideal or to let his individuality work by its own gravity, as it were. A conference of earnest Christian men have met at regular intervals for some years past to discuss the best methods of promoting the welfare and development of colored people in this country. Yet, strange as it may seem, they have never invited a colored man or even intimated that one would be welcome to take part in their deliberations. Their remedial contrivances are purely theoretical or empirical, therefore, and the whole machinery devoid of soul.

The second important oversight in my judgment is closely allied to this and probably grows out of it, and that is not developing Negro womanhood as an essential fundamental for the elevation of the race, and utilizing this agency in extending the work of the Church.

Of the first I have possibly already presumed to say too much since it does not strictly come within the province of my subject. However, Macaulay somewhere criticises the Church of England as not knowing how to use fanatics, and declares that had Ignatius Loyola been in the Anglican instead of the Roman communion, the Jesuits would have been schismatics instead of Catholics; and if the religious awakenings of the Wesleys had been in Rome, she would have shaven their heads, tied ropes around their waists, and sent them out under her own banner and blessing. Whether this be true or not, there is certainly a vast amount of force potential for Negro evangelization rendered latent, or worse, antagonistic by the halting, uncertain, I had almost said, *trimming* policy of the Church in the South. This may sound both presumptuous and ungrateful. It is mortifying, I know, to benevolent wisdom, after having spent itself in the execution of well conned theories for the ideal development of a particular work, to hear perhaps the weakest and humblest element of that work asking "what doest thou?"

Yet so it will be in life. The "thus far and no farther" pattern cannot be fitted to any growth in God's kingdom. The universal law of development is "onward and upward." It is God-given and inviolable. From the unfolding of the germ in the acorn to reach the sturdy oak, to the growth of a human soul into the full knowledge and likeness of its Creator, the breadth and scope of the movement in each and all are too grand, too mysterious, too like God himself, to be encompassed and locked down in human molds.

After all the Southern slave owners were right: either the very alphabet of intellectual growth must be forbidden and the Negro dealt with absolutely as a chattel having neither rights nor sensibilities; or else the clamps and irons of mental and moral, as well as civil compression must be riven asunder and the truly enfranchised soul led to the entrance of that boundless vista through which it is to toil upwards to its beckoning God as the buried seed germ to meet the sun.

A perpetual colored diaconate, carefully and kindly superintended by the white clergy; congregations of shiny faced peasants with their clean white aprons and sunbonnets catechised at regular intervals and taught to recite the creed, the Lord's prayer and the ten commandments—duty towards God and duty towards neighbor, surely such well tended sheep ought to be grateful to their shepherds and content in that station of life to which it pleased God to call them. True, like the old professor lecturing to his solitary student, we make no provision here for irregularities. "Questions must be kept till after class," or dispensed with altogether. That some do ask questions and insist on answers, in class too, must be both impertinent and annoying. Let not our spiritual pastors and masters however be grieved at such self-assertion as merely signifies we have a destiny to fulfill and as men and women we must *be about our Father's business*.

It is a mistake to suppose that the Negro is prejudiced against a white ministry. Naturally there is not a more kindly and implicit follower of a white man's guidance than the average colored peasant. What would to others be an ordinary act of friendly or pastoral interest he would be more inclined to regard gratefully as a condescension. And he never forgets such kindness. Could the Negro be brought near to his white priest or bishop, he is not suspicious. He is not only willing but often longs to unburden his soul to this intelligent guide. There are no reservations when he is convinced that you are his friend. It is a saddening satire on American history and manners that it takes something to convince him.

That our people are not "drawn" to a church whose chief dignitaries they see only in the chancel, and whom they reverence as they would a painting or an angel, whose life never comes down to and touches theirs with the inspiration of an objective reality, may be "perplexing" truly (American caste and American Christianity both being facts) but it need not be surprising. There must be something of human nature in it, the same as that which brought about that "the Word was made flesh and dwelt among us" that He might "draw" us towards God.

Men are not "drawn" by abstractions. Only sympathy and love can draw, and until our Church in America realizes this and provides a clergy that can come in touch with our life and have a fellow feeling for our woes, without being imbedded and frozen up in their "Gothic antipathies," the good bishops are likely to continue "perplexed" by the sparsity of colored Episcopalians.

A colored priest of my acquaintance recently related to me, with tears in his eyes, how his reverend Father in God, the Bishop who had ordained him, had met him on the cars on his way to the diocesan convention and warned him, not unkindly, not to take a seat in the body of the convention with the white clergy. To avoid disturbance of their godly placidity he would of course please sit back and somewhat apart. I do not imagine that that clergyman had very much heart for the Christly (!) deliberations of that convention.

To return, however, it is not on this broader view of Church work, which I mentioned as a primary cause of its halting progress with the colored people, that I am to speak. My proper theme is the second oversight of which in my judgment our Christian propagandists have been guilty: or, the necessity of church training, protecting and uplifting our colored womanhood as indispensable to the evangelization of the race.

Apelles did not disdain even that criticism of his lofty art which came from an uncouth cobbler; and may I not hope that the writer's oneness with her subject both in feeling and in being may palliate undue obtrusiveness of opinions here. That the race cannot be effectually lifted up till its women are truly elevated we take as proven. It is not for us to dwell on the needs, the neglects, and the ways of succor, pertaining to the black woman of the South. The ground has been ably discussed and an admirable and practical plan proposed by the oldest Negro priest in America, advising and urging that special organizations such as Church Sisterhoods and industrial schools be devised to meet her pressing needs in the Southland. That some such movements are vital to the life of this people and the extension of the Church among them, is not hard to see. Yet the pamphlet fell still-born from the press. So far as I am informed the Church has made no motion towards carrying out Dr. Crummell's suggestion.

The denomination which comes next our own in opposing the proverbial emotionalism of Negro worship in the South, and which in consequence like ours receives the cold shoulder from the old heads, resting as we do under the charge of not "having religion" and not believing in conversion—the Congregationalists—have quietly gone to work on the young, have established industrial and training schools, and now almost every community in the South is yearly enriched by a fresh infusion of vigorous young hearts, cultivated heads, and helpful hands that have been trained at Fisk, at Hampton, in Atlanta University, and in Tuskegee, Alabama.

These young people are missionaries actual or virtual both here and in Africa. They have learned to love the methods and doctrines of the Church which trained and educated them; and so Congregationalism surely and steadily progresses.

Need I compare these well known facts with results shown by the Church in the same field and during the same or even a longer time.

The institution of the Church in the South to which she mainly looks for the training of her colored clergy and for the help of the "Black Woman" and "Colored Girl" of the South, has graduated since the year 1868, when the school was founded, *five young women;** and while yearly numerous young men have been kept and trained for the ministry by the charities of the Church, the number of indigent females who have here been supported, sheltered and trained, is phenomenally small. Indeed, to my mind, the attitude of the Church toward this feature of her work is as if the solution of the problem of Negro missions depended solely on sending a quota of deacons and priests into the field, girls being a sort of *tertium quid* whose development may be promoted if they can pay their way and fall in with the plans mapped out for the training of the other sex. Now I would ask in all earnestness, does not this force potential deserve by education and stimulus to be made dynamic? Is it not a solemn duty incumbent on all colored churchmen to make it so? Will not the aid of the Church be given to prepare our girls in head, heart, and hand for the duties and responsibilities that await the intelligent wife, the Christian mother, the earnest, virtuous, helpful woman, at once both the lever and the fulcrum for uplifting the race.

As Negroes and churchmen we cannot be indifferent to these questions. They touch us most vitally on both sides. We believe in the Holy Catholic Church. We believe that however gigantic and

---

* Five have been graduated since '86, two in '91, two in '92.

apparently remote the consummation, the Church will go on conquering and to conquer till the kingdoms of this world, not except-
ing the black man and the black woman of the South, shall have
become the kingdoms of the Lord and of his Christ.

That past work in this direction has been unsatisfactory we must
admit. That without a change of policy results in the future will be
as meagre, we greatly fear. Our life as a race is at stake. The dearest
interests of our hearts are in the scales. We must either break away
from dear old landmarks and plunge out in any line and every line
that enables us to meet the pressing need of our people, or we must
ask the Church to allow and help us, untrammelled by the prejudices and theories of individuals, to work agressively under her
direction as we alone can, with God's help, for the salvation of our
people.

The time is ripe for action. Self-seeking and ambition must be
laid on the altar. The battle is one of sacrifice and hardship, but our
duty is plain. We have been recipients of missionary bounty in
some sort for twenty-one years. Not even the senseless vegetable is
content to be a mere reservoir. Receiving without giving is an
anomaly in nature. Nature's cells are all little workshops for manu-
facturing sunbeams, the product to be *given out* to earth's inhabitants
in warmth, energy, thought, action. Inanimate creation always pays
back an equivalent.

Now, *How much owest thou my Lord?* Will his account be overdrawn if he call for singleness of purpose and self-sacrificing labor for
your brethren? Having passed through your drill school, will you
refuse a general's commission even if it entail responsibility, risk and
anxiety, with possibly some adverse criticism? Is it too much to ask
you to step forward and direct the work for your race along those
lines which you know to be of first and vital importance?

Will you allow these words of Ralph Waldo Emerson? "In ordinary," says he, "we have a snappish criticism which watches and
contradicts the opposite party. We want the will which advances
and dictates [acts]. Nature has made up her mind that what cannot
defend itself, shall not be defended. Complaining never so loud and
with never so much reason, is of no use. What cannot stand must
fall; *and the measure of our sincerity and therefore of the respect of men is
the amount of health and wealth we will hazard in the defense of our right.*"

THE HIGHER EDUCATION OF WOMEN

IN THE VERY first year of our century, the year 1801, there appeared in Paris a book by Silvain Marechal, entitled "Shall Woman Learn the Alphabet." The book proposes a law prohibiting the alphabet to women, and quotes authorities weighty and various, to prove that the woman who knows the alphabet has already lost part of her womanliness. The author declares that woman can use the alphabet only as Moliere predicted they would, in spelling out the verb *amo;* that they have no occasion to peruse Ovid's *Ars Amoris,* since that is already the ground and limit of their intuitive furnishing; that Madame Guion would have been far more adorable had she remained a beautiful ignoramus as nature made her; that Ruth, Naomi, the Spartan woman, the Amazons, Penelope, Andromache, Lucretia, Joan of Arc, Petrarch's Laura, the daughters of Charlemagne, could not spell their names; while Sappho, Aspasia, Madame de Maintenon, and Madame de Stael could read altogether too well for their good; finally, that if women were once permitted to read Sophocles and work with logarithms, or to nibble at any side of the apple of knowledge, there would be an end forever to their sewing on buttons and embroidering slippers.

Please remember this book was published at the *beginning* of the Nineteenth Century. At the end of its first third, (in the year 1833) one solitary college in America decided to admit women within its sacred precincts, and organized what was called a "Ladies' Course" as well as the regular B. A. or Gentlemen's course.

It was felt to be an experiment—a rather dangerous experiment—and was adopted with fear and trembling by the good fathers, who looked as if they had been caught secretly mixing explosive compounds and were guiltily expecting every moment to see the foundations under them shaken and rent and their fair superstructure shattered into fragments.

But the girls came, and there was no upheaval. They performed their tasks modestly and intelligently. Once in a while one or two were found choosing the gentlemen's course. Still no collapse; and the dear, careful, scrupulous, frightened old professors were just getting their hearts out of their throats and preparing to draw one good free breath, when they found they would have to change the names of those courses; for there were as many ladies in the gentlemen's course as in the ladies', and a distinctively Ladies' Course, inferior in scope and aim to the regular classical course, did not and could not exist.

Other colleges gradually fell into line, and to-day there are one hundred and ninety-eight colleges for women, and two hundred and seven coeducational colleges and universities in the United States alone offering the degree of B. A. to women, and sending out yearly into the arteries of this nation a warm, rich flood of strong, brave, active, energetic, well-equipped, thoughtful women—women quick to see and eager to help the needs of this needy world—women who can think as well as feel, and who feel none the less because they think—women who are none the less tender and true for the parchment scroll they bear in their hands—women who have given a deeper, richer, nobler and grander meaning to the word "womanly" than any one-sided masculine definition could ever have suggested or inspired—women whom the world has long waited for in pain and anguish till there should be at last added to its forces and allowed to permeate its thought the complement of that masculine influence which has dominated it for fourteen centuries.

Since the idea of order and subordination succumbed to barbarian brawn and brutality in the fifth century, the civilized world has been like a child brought up by his father. It has needed the great mother heart to teach it to be pitiful, to love mercy, to succor the weak and care for the lowly.

Whence came this apotheosis of greed and cruelty? Whence this sneaking admiration we all have for bullies and prize-fighters? Whence the self-congratulation of "dominant" races, as if "dominant" meant "righteous" and carried with it a title to inherit the earth? Whence the scorn of so-called weak or unwarlike races and individuals, and the very comfortable assurance that it is their manifest destiny to be wiped out as vermin before this advancing civilization? As if the possession of the Christian graces of meekness, non-resistance and forgiveness, were incompatible with a civilization professedly based on Christianity, the religion of love! Just listen to this little bit of Barbarian brag:

"As for Far Orientals, they are not of those who will survive. Artistic attractive people that they are, their civilization is like their own tree flowers, beautiful blossoms destined never to bear fruit. If these people continue in their old course, their earthly career is closed. Just as surely as morning passes into afternoon, so surely are these races of the Far East, if unchanged, destined to disappear before the advancing nations of the West. Vanish, they will, off the face of the earth, and leave our planet the eventual possession of the dwellers where the day declines. Unless their newly imported ideas really take root, it is from this whole world that Japanese and Koreans, as well as Chinese, will inevitably be excluded. Their Nirvana is already being realized; already, it has wrapped Far Eastern Asia in its winding sheet."—*Soul of the Far East*—P. Lowell.

Delightful reflection for "the dwellers where day declines." A spectacle to make the gods laugh, truly, to see the scion of an upstart race by one sweep of his generalizing pen consigning to annihilation one-third the inhabitants of the globe—a people whose civilization was hoary headed before the parent elements that begot his race had advanced beyond nebulosity.

How like Longfellow's Iagoo, we Westerners are, to be sure! In the few hundred years, we have had to strut across our allotted territory and bask in the afternoon sun, we imagine we have exhausted the possibilities of humanity. Verily, we are the people, and after us there is none other. Our God is power; strength, our standard of excellence, inherited from barbarian ancestors through a long line of male progenitors, the Law Salic permitting no feminine modifications.

Says one, "The Chinaman is not popular with us, and we do not like the Negro. It is not that the eyes of the one are set bias, and the other is dark-skinned; but the Chinaman, the Negro is weak—*and Anglo Saxons don't like weakness*."

The world of thought under the predominant man-influence, unmollified and unrestrained by its complementary force, would become like Daniel's fourth beast: "dreadful and terrible, and *strong* exceedingly;" "it had great iron teeth; it devoured and brake in pieces, and stamped the residue with the feet of it;" and the most independent of us find ourselves ready at times to fall down and worship this incarnation of power.

Mrs. Mary A. Livermore, a woman whom I can mention only to admire, came near shaking my faith a few weeks ago in my theory of the thinking woman's mission to put in the tender and sympathetic chord in nature's grand symphony, and counteract, or better, harmonize the diapason of mere strength and might.

She was dwelling on the Anglo-Saxon genius for power and his contempt for weakness, and described a scene in San Francisco which she had witnessed.

The incorrigible animal known as the American small-boy, had pounced upon a simple, unoffending Chinaman, who was taking home his work, and had emptied the beautifully laundried contents of his basket into the ditch. "And," said she, "when that great man stood there and blubbered before that crowd of lawless urchins, to any one of whom he might have taught a lesson with his two fists, *I didn't much care.*"

This is said like a man! It grates harshly. It smacks of the worship of the beast. It is contempt for weakness, and taken out of its setting it seems to contradict my theory. It either shows that one of the highest exponents of the Higher Education can be at times untrue to the instincts I have ascribed to the thinking woman and to the contribution she is to add to the civilized world, or else the influence she wields upon our civilization may be potent without being necessarily and always direct and conscious. The latter is the case. Her voice may strike a false note, but her whole being is musical with the vibrations of human suffering. Her tongue may parrot over the cold conceits that some man has taught her, but her heart is aglow with sympathy and loving kindness, and she cannot be true to her real self without giving out these elements into the forces of the world.

No one is in any danger of imagining Mark Antony "a plain blunt man," nor Cassius a sincere one—whatever the speeches they may make.

As individuals, we are constantly and inevitably, whether we are conscious of it or not, giving out our real selves into our several little worlds, inexorably adding our own true ray to the flood of starlight, quite independently of our professions and our masquerading; and so in the world of thought, the influence of thinking woman far transcends her feeble declamation and may seem at times even opposed to it.

A visitor in Oberlin once said to the lady principal, "Have you no rabble in Oberlin? How is it I see no police here, and yet the streets are as quiet and orderly as if there were an officer of the law standing on every corner."

Mrs. Johnston replied, "Oh, yes; there are vicious persons in Oberlin just as in other towns—*but our girls are our police.*"

With from five to ten hundred pure-minded young women threading the streets of the village every evening unattended, vice must slink away, like frost before the rising sun: and yet I venture to say there was not one in a hundred of those girls who would not have run from a street brawl as she would from a mouse, and who would not have declared she could never stand the sight of blood and pistols.

There is, then, a real and special influence of woman. An influence subtle and often involuntary, an influence so intimately interwoven in, so intricately interpenetrated by the masculine influence of the time that it is often difficult to extricate the delicate meshes and analyze and identify the closely clinging fibers. And yet, without this influence—so long as woman sat with bandaged eyes and manacled hands, fast bound in the clamps of ignorance and inaction, the world of thought moved in its orbit like the revolutions of the moon; with one face (the man's face) always out, so that the spectator could not distinguish whether it was disc or sphere.

Now I claim that it is the prevalence of the Higher Education among women, the making it a common everyday affair for women to reason and think and express their thought, the training and stimulus which enable and encourage women to administer to the world the bread it needs as well as the sugar it cries for; in short it is the transmitting the potential forces of her soul into dynamic factors that has given symmetry and completeness to the world's agencies. So only could it be consummated that Mercy, the lesson she teaches, and Truth, the task man has set himself, should meet together: that righteousness, or *rightness*, man's ideal,—and *peace,* its necessary 'other half,' should kiss each other.

We must thank the general enlightenment and independence of woman (which we may now regard as a *fait accompli*) that both these forces are now at work in the world, and it is fair to demand from them for the twentieth century a higher type of civilization than any

attained in the nineteenth. Religion, science, art, economics, have all
needed the feminine flavor; and literature, the expression of what is
permanent and best in all of these, may be gauged at any time to
measure the strength of the feminine ingredient. You will not find
theology consigning infants to lakes of unquenchable fire long after
women have had a chance to grasp, master, and wield its dogmas.
You will not find science annihilating personality from the government of the Universe and making of God an ungovernable, unintel-
ligible, blind, often destructive physical force; you will not find
jurisprudence formulating as an axiom the absurdity that man and
wife are one, and that one the man—that the married woman may
not hold or bequeath her own property save as subject to her husband's direction; you will not find political economists declaring that
the only possible adjustment between laborers and capitalists is that of
selfishness and rapacity—that each must get all he can and keep all
that he gets, while the world cries *laissez faire* and the lawyers explain,
"it is the beautiful working of the law of supply and demand;" in
fine, you will not find the law of love shut out from the affairs of men
after the feminine half of the world's truth is completed.

Nay, put your ear now close to the pulse of the time. What is
the key-note of the literature of these days? What is the banner cry
of all the activities of the last half decade? What is the dominant
seventh which is to add richness and tone to the final cadences of
this century and lead by a grand modulation into the triumphant
harmonies of the next? Is it not compassion for the poor and
unfortunate, and, as Bellamy has expressed it, "indignant outcry
against the failure of the social machinery as it is, to ameliorate the
miseries of men!" Even Christianity is being brought to the bar of
humanity and tried by the standard of its ability to alleviate the
world's suffering and lighten and brighten its woe. What else can
be the meaning of Matthew Arnold's saddening protest, "We cannot do without Christianity," cried he, "and we cannot endure it
as it is."

When went there by an age, when so much time and thought, so
much money and labor were given to God's poor and God's invalids, the lowly and unlovely, the sinning as well as the suffering—
homes for inebriates and homes for lunatics, shelter for the aged
and shelter for babes, hospitals for the sick, props and braces for the
falling, reformatory prisons and prison reformatories, all show that
a "mothering" influence from some source is leavening the nation.

Now please understand me. I do not ask you to admit that these
benefactions and virtues are the exclusive possession of women, or
even that women are their chief and only advocates. It may be a man
who formulates and makes them vocal. It may be, and often is, a man
who weeps over the wrongs and struggles for the amelioration: but
that man has imbibed those impulses from a mother rather than from
a father and is simply materializing and giving back to the world in
tangible form the ideal love and tenderness, devotion and care that
have cherished and nourished the helpless period of his own existence.

All I claim is that there is a feminine as well as a masculine side to
truth; that these are related not as inferior and superior, not as better
and worse, not as weaker and stronger, but as complements—
complements in one necessary and symmetric whole. That as the
man is more noble in reason, so the woman is more quick in sympathy. That as he is indefatigable in pursuit of abstract truth, so is she
in caring for the interests by the way—striving tenderly and lovingly
that not one of the least of these 'little ones' should perish. That
while we not unfrequently see women who reason, we say, with the
coolness and precision of a man, and men as considerate of helplessness as a woman, still there is a general consensus of mankind that
the one trait is essentially masculine and the other as peculiarly
feminine. That both are needed to be worked into the training of
children, in order that our boys may supplement their virility by
tenderness and sensibility, and our girls may round out their gentleness by strength and self-reliance. That, as both are alike necessary
in giving symmetry to the individual, so a nation or a race will
degenerate into mere emotionalism on the one hand, or bullyism on
the other, if dominated by either exclusively; lastly, and most
emphatically, that the feminine factor can have its proper effect only
through woman's development and education so that she may fitly
and intelligently stamp her force on the forces of her day, and add
her modicum to the riches of the world's thought.

> "For woman's cause is man's: they rise or sink
> Together, dwarfed or godlike, bond or free:
> For she that out of Lethe scales with man
> The shining steps of nature, shares with man
> His nights, his days, moves with him to one goal.
> If she be small, slight-natured, miserable,
> How shall men grow?

   ★   ★   ★   Let her make herself her own
To give or keep, to live and learn and be
All that not harms distinctive womanhood.
For woman is not undeveloped man
But diverse: could we make her as the man
Sweet love were slain; his dearest bond is this,
Not like to like, but like in difference.
Yet in the long years liker must they grow;
The man be more of woman, she of man;
He gain in sweetness and in moral height,
Nor lose the wrestling thews that throw the world;
She mental breadth, nor fail in childward care,
Nor lose the childlike in the larger mind;
Till at the last she set herself to man,
Like perfect music unto noble words."

Now you will argue, perhaps, and rightly, that higher education for women is not a modern idea, and that, if that is the means of setting free and invigorating the long desired feminine force in the world, it has already had a trial and should, in the past, have produced some of these glowing effects. Sappho, the bright, sweet singer of Lesbos, "the violet-crowned, pure, sweetly smiling Sappho" as Alcaeus calls her, chanted her lyrics and poured forth her soul nearly six centuries before Christ, in notes as full and free, as passionate and eloquent as did ever Archilochus or Anacreon.

Aspasia, that earliest queen of the drawing-room, a century later ministered to the intellectual entertainment of Socrates and the leading wits and philosophers of her time. Indeed, to her is attributed, by the best critics, the authorship of one of the most noted speeches ever delivered by Pericles.

Later on, during the Renaissance period, women were professors in mathematics, physics, metaphysics, and the classic languages in Bologna, Pavia, Padua, and Brescia. Olympia Fulvia Morata, of Ferrara, a most interesting character, whose magnificent library was destroyed in 1553 in the invasion of Schweinfurt by Albert of Brandenburg, had acquired a most extensive education. It is said that this wonderful girl gave lectures on classical subjects in her sixteenth year, and had even before that written several very remarkable Greek and Latin poems, and what is also to the point, she married a professor at Heidelberg, and became a *help-meet for him.*

It is true then that the higher education for women—in fact, the highest that the world has ever witnessed—belongs to the past; but we must remember that it was possible, down to the middle of our own century, only to a select few; and that the fashions and traditions of the times were before that all against it. There were not only no stimuli to encourage women to make the most of their powers and to welcome their development as a helpful agency in the progress of civilization, but their little aspirations, when they had any, were chilled and snubbed in embryo, and any attempt at thought was received as a monstrous usurpation of man's prerogative.

Lessing declared that "the woman who thinks is like the man who puts on rouge—ridiculous;" and Voltaire in his coarse, flippant way used to say, "Ideas are like beards—women and boys have none." Dr. Maginn remarked, "We like to hear a few words of sense from a woman sometimes, as we do from a parrot—they are so unexpected!" and even the pious Fenelon taught that virgin delicacy is almost as incompatible with learning as with vice.

That the average woman retired before these shafts of wit and ridicule and even gloried in her ignorance is not surprising. The Abbe Choisi, it is said, praised the Duchesse de Fontanges as being pretty as an angel and silly as a goose, and all the young ladies of the court strove to make up in folly what they lacked in charms. The ideal of the day was that "women must be pretty, dress prettily, flirt prettily, and not be too well informed;" that it was the *summum bonum* of her earthly hopes to have, as Thackeray puts it, "all the fellows battling to dance with her;" that she had no God-given destiny, no soul with unquenchable longings and inexhaustible possibilities—no work of her own to do and give to the world— no absolute and inherent value, no duty to self, transcending all pleasure-giving that may be demanded of a mere toy; but that her value was purely a relative one and to be estimated as are the fine arts—by the pleasure they give. "Woman, wine and song," as "the world's best gifts to man," were linked together in praise with as little thought of the first saying, "What doest thou," as that the wine and the song should declare, "We must be about our Father's business."

Men believed, or pretended to believe, that the great law of self development was obligatory on their half of the human family only; that while it was the chief end of man to glorify God and put his five talents to the exchangers, gaining thereby other five, it was, or ought to be, the sole end of woman to glorify man and wrap her one decently away in a napkin, retiring into "Hezekiah Smith's lady during her natural life and Hezekiah Smith's relict on her tombstone;" that higher education was incompatible with the shape of the female cerebrum, and that even if it could be acquired it must inevitably unsex woman destroying the lisping, clinging, tenderly helpless, and beautifully dependent creatures whom men would so heroically think for and so gallantly fight for, and giving in their stead a formidable race of blue stockings with corkscrew ringlets and other spinster propensities.

But these are eighteenth century ideas.

We have seen how the pendulum has swung across our present century. The men of our time have asked with Emerson, "that woman only show us how she can best be served;" and woman has replied: the chance of the seedling and of the animalcule is all I ask—the chance for growth and self development, the permission to be true to the aspirations of my soul without incurring the blight of your censure and ridicule.

"Audetque viris concurrere virgo."

In soul-culture woman at last dares to contend with men, and we may cite Grant Allen (who certainly cannot be suspected of advocating the unsexing of woman) as an example of the broadening effect of this contest on the ideas at least of the men of the day. He says in his *Plain Words on the Woman Question*, recently published:

"The position of woman was not [in the past a] position which could bear the test of nineteenth-century scrutiny. Their education was inadequate, their social status was humiliating, their political power was nil, their practical and personal grievances were innumerable; above all, their relations to the family—to their husbands, their children, their friends, their property—was simply insupportable."

And again: "As a body we 'Advanced men' are, I think, prepared to reconsider, and to reconsider fundamentally, without prejudice or misconception, the entire question of the relation betwen the sexes. We are ready to make any modifications in those relations which will satisfy the woman's just aspiration for personal independence, for intellectual and moral development, for physical culture, for political activity, and for a voice in the arrangement of her own affairs, both domestic and national."

Now this is magnanimous enough, surely; and quite a step from eighteenth century preaching, is it not? The higher education of Woman has certainly developed the men;—let us see what it has done for the women.

Matthew Arnold during his last visit to America in '82 or '83, lectured before a certain co-educational college in the West. After the lecture he remarked, with some surprise, to a lady professor, that the young women in his audience, he noticed, "paid as close attention as the men, *all the way through.*" This led, of course, to a spirited discussion of the higher education for women, during which he said to his enthusiastic interlocutor, eyeing her philosophically through his English eyeglass: "But—eh—don't you think it—eh—spoils their *chawnces*, you know!"

Now, as to the result to women, this is the most serious argument ever used against the higher education. If it interferes with marriage, classical training has a grave objection to weigh and answer.

For I agree with Mr. Allen at least on this one point, that there must be marrying and giving in marriage even till the end of time.

I grant you that intellectual development, with the self-reliance and capacity for earning a livelihood which it gives, renders woman less dependent on the marriage relation for physical support (which, by the way, does not always accompany it). Neither is she compelled to look to sexual love as the one sensation capable of giving tone and relish, movement and vim to the life she leads. Her horizon is extended. Her sympathies are broadened and deepened and multiplied. She is in closer touch with nature. Not a bud that opens, not a dew drop, not a ray of light, not a cloud-burst or a thunderbolt, but adds to the expansiveness and zest of her soul. And if the sun of an absorbing passion be gone down, still 'tis night that brings the stars. She has remaining the mellow, less obtrusive, but none the less enchanting and inspiring light of friendship, and into its charmed circle she may gather the best the world has known. She can commune with Socrates about the *daimon* he knew and to which she too can bear witness; she can revel in the majesty of Dante, the sweetness of Virgil, the simplicity of Homer, the strength of Milton. She can listen to the pulsing heart throbs of passionate Sappho's encaged soul, as she beats her bruised wings against her prison bars and struggles to flutter out into Heaven's æther, and the fires of her own soul cry back as she listens. "Yes; Sappho, I know it all; I know it all." Here, at last, can be communion without suspicion; friendship without misunderstanding; love without jealousy.

We must admit then that Byron's picture, whether a thing of beauty or not, has faded from the canvas of to-day.

"Man's love," he wrote, "is of man's life a thing apart,
'Tis woman's whole existence.
Man may range the court, camp, church, the vessel and the mart,
Sword, gown, gain, glory offer in exchange.
Pride, fame, ambition, to fill up his heart—
And few there are whom these cannot estrange.
Men have all these resources, we *but one*—
To love again and be again undone."

This may have been true when written. *It is not true to-day*. The old, subjective, stagnant, indolent and wretched life for woman has gone. She has as many resources as men, as many activities beckon her on. As large possibilities swell and inspire her heart.

Now, then, does it destroy or diminish her capacity for loving?

Her standards have undoubtedly gone up. The necessity of speculating in 'chawnces' has probably shifted. The question is not now with the woman "How shall I so cramp, stunt, simplify and nullify myself as to make me elegible to the honor of being swallowed up into some little man?" but the problem, I trow, now rests with the man as to how he can so develop his God-given powers as to reach the ideal of a generation of women who demand the noblest, grandest and best achievements of which he is capable; and this surely is the only fair and natural adjustment of the chances. Nature never meant that the ideals and standards of the world should be dwarfing and minimizing ones, and the men should thank us for requiring of them the richest fruits which they can grow. If it makes them work, all the better for them.

As to the adaptability of the educated woman to the marriage relation, I shall simply quote from that excellent symposium of learned women that appeared recently under Mrs. Armstrong's signature in answer to the "Plain Words" of Mr. Allen, already referred to. "Admitting no longer any question as to their intellectual equality with the men whom they meet, with the simplicity of conscious strength, they take their place beside the men who challenge them, and fearlessly face the result of their actions. They deny that their education in any way unfits them for the duty of wifehood and maternity or primarily renders these conditions any less attractive to them than to the domestic type of woman. On the contrary, they hold that their knowledge of physiology makes them better mothers and housekeepers; their knowledge of chemistry makes them better cooks; while from their training in other natural sciences and in mathematics, they obtain an accuracy and fair-mindedness which is of great value to them in dealing with their children or employees."

So much for their willingness. Now the apple may be good for food and pleasant to the eyes, and a fruit to be desired to make one wise. Nay, it may even assure you that it has no aversion whatever to being tasted. Still, if you do not like the flavor all these recommendations are nothing. Is the intellectual woman *desirable* in the matrimonial market?

This I cannot answer. I confess my ignorance. I am no judge of such things. I have been told that strong-minded women could be, when they thought it worth their while, quite endurable, and, judging from the number of female names I find in college catalogues among the alumnae with double patronymics, I surmise that quite a number of men are willing to put up with them.

Now I would that my task ended here. Having shown that a great want of the world in the past has been a feminine force; that that force can have its full effect only through the untrammelled development of woman; that such development, while it gives her to the world and to civilization, does not necessarily remove her from the home and fireside; finally, that while past centuries have witnessed sporadic instances of this higher growth, still it was reserved for the latter half of the nineteenth century to render it common and general enough to be effective; I might close with a glowing prediction of what the twentieth century may expect from this heritage of twin forces—the masculine battered and toil-worn as a grim veteran after centuries of warfare, but still strong, active, and vigorous, ready to help with his hard-won experience the young recruit rejoicing in her newly found freedom, who so confidently places her hand in his with mutual pledges to redeem the ages.

> "And so the twain upon the skirts of Time,
>   Sit side by side, full-summed in all their powers,

Dispensing harvest, sowing the To-be,
Self-reverent each and reverencing each."

Fain would I follow them, but duty is nearer home. The high ground of generalities is alluring but my pen is devoted to a special cause: and with a view to further enlightenment on the achievements of the century for THE HIGHER EDUCATION OF COLORED WOMEN, I wrote a few days ago to the colleges which admit women and asked how many colored women had completed the B. A. course in each during its entire history. These are the figures returned: Fisk leads the way with twelve; Oberlin next with five; Wilberforce, four; Ann Arbor and Wellesley three each, Livingstone two, Atlanta one, Howard, as yet, none.

I then asked the principal of the Washington High School how many out of a large number of female graduates from his school had chosen to go forward and take a collegiate course. He replied that but one had ever done so, and she was then in Cornell.*

Others ask questions too, sometimes, and I was asked a few years ago by a white friend, "How is it that the men of your race seem to outstrip the women in mental attainment?" "Oh," I said, "so far as it is true, the men, I suppose, from the life they lead, gain more by contact; and so far as it is only apparent, I think the women are more quiet. They don't feel called to mount a barrel and harangue by the hour every time they imagine they have produced an idea."

But I am sure there is another reason which I did not at that time see fit to give. The atmosphere, the standards, the requirements of our little world do not afford any special stimulus to female development.

It seems hardly a gracious thing to say, but it strikes me as true, that while our men seem thoroughly abreast of the times on almost every other subject, when they strike the woman question they drop back into sixteenth century logic. They leave nothing to be desired generally in regard to gallantry and chivalry, but they actually do not seem sometimes to have outgrown that old contemporary of chivalry—the idea that women may stand on pedestals or live in doll houses, (if they happen to have them) but they must not furrow

---

* Graduated from Scientific Course, June, 1890, the first colored woman to graduate from Cornell.

their brows with thought or attempt to help men tug at the great questions of the world. I fear the majority of colored men do not yet think it worth while that women aspire to higher education. Not many will subscribe to the "advanced" ideas of Grant Allen already quoted. The three R's, a little music and a good deal of dancing, a first rate dress-maker and a bottle of magnolia balm, are quite enough generally to render charming any woman possessed of tact and the capacity for worshipping masculinity.

My readers will pardon my illustrating my point and also giving a reason for the fear that is in me, by a little bit of personal experience. When a child I was put into a school near home that professed to be normal and collegiate, i.e. to prepare teachers for colored youth, furnish candidates for the ministry, and offer collegiate training for those who should be ready for it. Well, I found after a while that I had a good deal of time on my hands. I had devoured what was put before me, and, like Oliver Twist, was looking around to ask for more. I constantly felt (as I suppose many an ambitious girl has felt) a thumping from within unanswered by any beckoning from without. Class after class was organized for these ministerial candidates (many of them men who had been preaching before I was born). Into every one of these classes I was expected to go, with the sole intent, I thought at the time, of enabling the dear old principal, as he looked from the vacant countenances of his sleepy old class over to where I sat, to get off his solitary pun—his never-failing pleasantry, especially in hot weather—which was, as he called out "Any one!" to the effect that "*any* one" then meant "*Annie* one."

Finally a Greek class was to be formed. My inspiring preceptor informed me that Greek had never been taught in the school, but that he was going to form a class *for the candidates for the ministry*, and if I liked I might join it. I replied—humbly I hope, as became a female of the human species—that I would like very much to study Greek, and that I was thankful for the opportunity, and so it went on. A boy, however meager his equipment and shallow his pretentions, had only to declare a floating intention to study theology and he could get all the support, encouragement and stimulus he needed, be absolved from work and invested beforehand with all the dignity of his far away office. While a self-supporting girl had to struggle on by teaching in the summer and working after school hours to keep up with her board bills, and actually to fight her way against positive discouragements to the higher education; till one such girl one day flared out and told the principal "the only mission opening before a girl in his school was to marry one of those candidates." He said he didn't know but it was. And when at last that same girl announced her desire and intention to go to college it was received with about the same incredulity and dismay as if a brass button on one of those candidate's coats had propounded a new method for squaring the circle or trisecting the arc.

Now this is not fancy. It is a simple unvarnished photograph, and what I believe was not in those days exceptional in colored schools, and I ask the men and women who are teachers and co-workers for the highest interests of the race, that they give the girls a chance! We might as well expect to grow trees from leaves as hope to build up a civilization or a manhood without taking into consideration our women and the home life made by them, which must be the root and ground of the whole matter. Let us insist then on special encouragement for the education of our women and special care in their training. Let our girls feel that we expect something more of them than that they merely look pretty and appear well in society. Teach them that there is a race with special needs which they and only they can help; that the world needs and is already asking for their trained, efficient forces. Finally, if there is an ambitious girl with pluck and brain to take the higher education, encourage her to make the most of it. Let there be the same flourish of trumpets and clapping of hands as when a boy announces his determination to enter the lists; and then, as you know that she is physically the weaker of the two, don't stand from under and leave her to buffet the waves alone. Let her know that your heart is following her, that your hand, though she sees it not, is ready to support her. To be plain, I mean let money be raised and scholarships be founded in our colleges and universities for self-supporting, worthy young women, to offset and balance the aid that can always be found for boys who will take theology.

The earnest well trained Christian young woman, as a teacher, as a home-maker, as wife, mother, or silent influence even, is as potent a missionary agency among our people as is the theologian; and I claim that at the present stage of our development in the South she is even more important and necessary.

Let us then, here and now, recognize this force and resolve to make the most of it—not the boys less, but the girls more.

"WOMAN VERSUS THE INDIAN"

In the National Woman's Council convened at Washington in February 1891, among a number of thoughtful and suggestive papers read by eminent women, was one by the Rev. Anna Shaw, bearing the above title.

That Miss Shaw is broad and just and liberal in principle is proved beyond contradiction. Her noble generosity and womanly firmness are unimpeachable. The unwavering stand taken by herself and Miss Anthony in the subsequent color ripple in Wimodaughsis ought to be sufficient to allay forever any doubts as to the pure gold of these two women.

Of Wimodaughsis (which, being interpreted for the uninitiated, is a woman's culture club whose name is made up of the first few letters of the four words wives, mothers, daughters, and sisters) Miss Shaw is president, and a lady from the Blue Grass State *was* secretary.

Pandora's box is opened in the ideal harmony of this modern Eden without an Adam when a colored lady, a teacher in one of our schools, applies for admission to its privileges and opportunities.

The Kentucky secretary, a lady zealous in good works and one who, I can't help imagining, belongs to that estimable class who daily thank the Lord that He made the earth that they may have the job of superintending its rotations, and who really would like to help "elevate" the colored people (in her own way of course and so long as they understand their places) is filled with grief and horror that any persons of Negro extraction should aspire to learn type-writing or languages or to enjoy any other advantages offered in the sacred halls of Wimodaughsis. Indeed, she had not calculated that there were any wives, mothers, daughters, and sisters, except white ones; and she is really convinced that *Whimodaughsis* would sound just as well, and then it need mean just *white mothers, daughters and sisters*. In fact, so far as there is anything in a name, nothing

36

would be lost by omitting for the sake of euphony, from this unique mosaic, the letters that represent wives. *Whiwimodaughsis* might be a little startling, and on the whole wives would better yield to white; since clearly all women are not wives, while surely all wives are daughters. The daughters therefore could represent the wives and this immaculate assembly for propagating liberal and progressive ideas and disseminating a broad and humanizing culture might be spared the painful possibility of the sight of a black man coming in the future to escort from an evening class this solitary cream-colored applicant. Accordingly the Kentucky secretary took the cream-colored applicant aside, and, with emotions befitting such an epoch-making crisis, told her, "as kindly as she could," that colored people were not admitted to the classes, at the same time refunding the money which said cream-colored applicant had paid for lessons in type-writing.

When this little incident came to the knowledge of Miss Shaw, she said firmly and emphatically, NO. As a minister of the gospel and as a Christian woman, she could not lend her influence to such unreasonable and uncharitable discrimination; and she must resign the honor of president of Wimodaughsis if persons were to be proscribed solely on account of their color.

To the honor of the board of managers, be it said, they sustained Miss Shaw; and the Kentucky secretary, and those whom she succeeded in inoculating with her prejudices, resigned.

'Twas only a ripple,—some bewailing of lost opportunity on the part of those who could not or would not seize God's opportunity for broadening and enlarging their own souls—and then the work flowed on as before.

Susan B. Anthony and Anna Shaw are evidently too noble to be held in thrall by the provincialisms of women who seem never to have breathed the atmosphere beyond the confines of their grandfathers' plantations. It is only from the broad plateau of light and love that one can see petty prejudice and narrow priggishness in their true perspective; and it is on this high ground, as I sincerely believe, these two grand women stand.

As leaders in the woman's movement of today, they have need of clearness of vision as well as firmness of soul in adjusting recalcitrant forces, and wheeling into line the thousand and one nonesuch, never-to-be-modified, won't-be-dictated-to banners of their somewhat mottled array.

The black woman and the southern woman, I imagine, often get them into the predicament of the befuddled man who had to take singly across a stream a bag of corn, a fox and a goose. There was no one to help, and to leave the goose with the fox was death—with the corn, destruction. To re-christen the animals, the lion could not be induced to lie down with the lamb unless the lamb would take the inside berth.

The black woman appreciates the situation and can even sympathize with the actors in the serio-comic dilemma.

But, may it not be that, as women, the very lessons which seem hardest to master now, are possibly the ones most essential for our promotion to a higher grade of work?

We assume to be leaders of thought and guardians of society. Our country's manners and morals are under our tutoring. Our standards are law in our several little worlds. However tenaciously men may guard some prerogatives, they are our willing slaves in that sphere which they have always conceded to be woman's. Here, no one dares demur when her fiat has gone forth. The man would be mad who presumed, however inexplicable and past finding out any reason for her action might be, to attempt to open a door in her kingdom officially closed and regally sealed by her.

The American woman of to-day not only gives tone directly to her immediate world, but her tiniest pulsation ripples out and out, down and down, till the outermost circles and the deepest layers of society feel the vibrations. It is pre-eminently an age of organizations. The "leading woman," the preacher, the reformer, the organizer "enthuses" her lieutenants and captains, the literary women, the thinking women, the strong, earnest, irresistible women; these in turn touch their myriads of church clubs, social clubs, culture clubs, pleasure clubs and charitable clubs, till the same lecture has been duly administered to every married man in the land (not to speak of sons and brothers) from the President in the White House to the stone-splitter of the ditches. And so woman's lightest whisper is heard as in Dionysius' ear, by quick relays and endless reproductions, through every recess and cavern as well as on every hilltop and mountain in her vast domain. And her mandates are obeyed. When she says "thumbs up," woe to the luckless thumb that falters in its rising. They may be little things, the amenities of life, the little nothings which cost nothing and come to nothing, and yet can make a sentient being so comfortable or so miserable in this life, the oil of social machinery, which we call the courtesies of life, all are under the magic key of woman's permit.

The American woman then is responsible for American manners. Not merely the right ascension and declination of the satellites of her own drawing room; but the rising and the setting of the pestilential or life-giving orbs which seem to wander afar in space, all are governed almost wholly through her magnetic polarity. The atmosphere of street cars and parks and boulevards, of cafes and hotels and steamboats is charged and surcharged with her sentiments and restrictions. Shop girls and serving maids, cashiers and accountant clerks, scribblers and drummers, whether wage earner, salaried toiler, or proprietress, whether laboring to instruct minds, to save souls, to delight fancies, or to win bread,—the working women of America in whatever station or calling they may be found, are subjects, officers, or rulers of a strong centralized government, and bound together by a system of codes and countersigns, which, though unwritten, forms a network of perfect subordination and unquestioning obedience as marvelous as that of the Jesuits. At the head and center in this regime stands the Leading Woman in the principality. The one talismanic word that plays along the wires from palace to cook-shop, from imperial Congress to the distant plain, is *Caste*. With all her vaunted independence, the American woman of to-day is as fearful of losing caste as a Brahmin in India. That is the law under which she lives, the precepts which she binds as frontlets between her eyes and writes on the door-posts of her homes, the lesson which she instils into her children with their first baby breakfasts, the injunction she lays upon husband and lover with direst penalties attached.

The queen of the drawing room is absolute ruler under this law. Her pose gives the cue. The microscopic angle at which her pencilled brows are elevated, signifies who may be recognized and who are beyond the pale. The delicate intimation is, quick as electricity, telegraphed down. Like the wonderful transformation in the House that Jack Built (or regions thereabouts) when the rat began to gnaw the rope, the rope to hang the butcher, the butcher to kill the ox, the ox to drink the water, the water to quench the fire, the fire to burn the stick, the stick to beat the dog, and the dog to worry the cat, and on, and on, and on,—when miladi causes the inner arch over her matchless orbs to ascend the merest trifle, *presto!* the Miss at the notions counter grows curt and pert, the dress goods clerk becomes indifferent and taciturn, hotel waiters and ticket dispensers look the other way, the Irish street laborer snarls and scowls, conductors, policemen and park superintendents jostle and push and threaten, and society suddenly seems transformed into a band of organized adders, snapping, and striking and hissing just because they like it on general principles. The tune set by the head singer, sung through all keys and registers, with all qualities of tone,—the smooth, flowing, and gentle, the creaking, whizzing, grating, screeching, growling—according to ability, taste, and temperament of the singers. Another application of like master, like man. In this case, like mistress, like nation.

It was the good fortune of the Black Woman of the South to spend some weeks, not long since, in a land over which floated the Union Jack. The Stars and Stripes were not the only familiar experiences missed. A uniform, matter-of-fact courtesy, a genial kindliness, quick perception of opportunities for rendering any little manly assistance, a readiness to give information to strangers,—a hospitable, thawing-out atmosphere everywhere—in shops and waiting rooms, on cars and in the streets, actually seemed to her chilled little soul to transform the commonest boor in the service of the public into one of nature's noblemen, and when the old whipped-cur feeling was taken up and analyzed she could hardly tell whether it consisted mostly of self pity for her own wounded sensibilities, or of shame for her country and mortification that her countrymen offered such an unfavorable contrast.

Some American girls, I noticed recently, in search of novelty and adventure, were taking an extended trip through our country unattended by gentleman friends; their wish was to write up for a periodical or lecture the ease and facility, the comfort and safety of American travel, even for the weak and unprotected, under our well-nigh perfect railroad systems and our gentlemanly and efficient corps of officials and public servants. I have some material I could furnish these young ladies, though possibly it might not be just on the side they wish to have illuminated. The Black Woman of the South has to do considerable travelling in this country, often unattended. She thinks she is quiet and unobtrusive in her manner, simple and inconspicuous in her dress, and can see no reason why in any chance assemblage of *ladies*, or even a promiscuous gathering of ordinarily well-bred and dignified individuals, she should be signaled out for any marked consideration. And yet she has seen these same "gentlemanly and efficient" railroad conductors, when their cars had stopped at stations having no raised platforms, making it necessary for passengers to take the long and trying leap from the car step to the ground or step on the narrow little stool placed under by the conductor, after standing at their posts and handing woman after woman from the steps to the stool, thence to the ground, or else relieving her of satchels and bags and enabling her to make the descent easily, deliberately fold their arms and turn round when the Black Woman's turn came to alight—bearing her satchel, and bearing besides another unnamable burden inside the heaving bosom and tightly compressed lips. The feeling of slighted womanhood is unlike every other emotion of the soul. Happily for the human family, it is unknown to many and indescribable to all. Its poignancy, compared with which even Juno's *spretae injuria formae* is earthly and vulgar, is holier than that of jealousy, deeper than indignation, tenderer than rage. Its first impulse of wrathful protest and proud self vindication is checked and shamed by the consciousness that self assertion would outrage still further the same delicate instinct. Were there a brutal attitude of hate or of ferocious attack, the feminine response of fear or repulsion is simple and spontaneous. But when the keen sting comes through the finer sensibilities, from a hand which, by all known traditions and ideals of propriety, should have been trained to reverence and respect them, the condemnation of man's inhumanity to woman is increased and embittered by the knowledge of personal identity with a race of beings so fallen.

I purposely forbear to mention instances of personal violence to colored women travelling in less civilized sections of our country, where women have been forcibly ejected from cars, thrown out of seats, their garments rudely torn, their person wantonly and cruelly injured. America is large and must for some time yet endure its out-of-the-way jungles of barbarism as Africa its uncultivated tracts of marsh and malaria. There are murderers and thieves and villains in both London and Paris. Humanity from the first has had its vultures and sharks, and representatives of the fraternity who prey upon mankind may be expected no less in America than elsewhere. That this virulence breaks out most readily and commonly against colored persons in this country, is due of course to the fact that they are, generally speaking, weak and can be imposed upon with impunity. Bullies are always cowards at heart and may be credited with a pretty safe instinct in scenting their prey. Besides, society, where it has not

exactly said to its dogs "s-s-sik him!" has at least engaged to be looking in another direction or studying the rivers on Mars. It is not of
the dogs and their doings, but of society holding the leash that I shall
speak. It is those subtle exhalations of atmospheric odors for which
woman is accountable, the indefinable, unplaceable aroma which
seems to exude from the very pores in her finger tips like the delicate sachet so dexterously hidden and concealed in her linens; the
essence of her teaching, guessed rather than read, so adroitly is the
lettering and wording manipulated; it is the undertones of the picture laid finely on by woman's own practiced hand, the reflection of
the lights and shadows on her own brow; it is, in a word, the repu-
tation of our nation for general politeness and good manners and of
our fellow citizens to be somewhat more than cads or snobs that
shall engage our present study. There can be no true test of national
courtesy without travel. Impressions and conclusions based on provincial traits and characteristics can thus be modified and general-
ized. Moreover, the weaker and less influential the experimenter,
the more exact and scientific the deductions. Courtesy "for revenue
only" is not politeness, but diplomacy. Any rough can assume civilty
toward those of "his set," and does not hesitate to carry it even to
servility toward those in whom he recognizes a possible patron or
his master in power, wealth, rank, or influence. But, as the chemist
prefers distilled H_2O in testing solutions to avoid complications and
unwarranted reactions, so the Black Woman holds that her feminin-
ity linked with the impossibility of popular affinity or unexpected
attraction through position and influence in her case makes her a
touchstone of American courtesy exceptionally pure and singularly
free from extraneous modifiers. The man who is courteous to her is
so, not because of anything he hopes or fears or sees, but because *he
is a gentleman.*

I would eliminate also from the discussion all uncharitable reflec-
tions upon the orderly execution of laws existing in certain states of
this Union, requiring persons known to be colored to ride in one
car, and persons supposed to be white in another. A good citizen
may use his influence to have existing laws and statutes changed or
modified, but a public servant must not be blamed for obeying
orders. A railroad conductor is not asked to dictate measures, nor to
make and pass laws. His bread and butter are conditioned on his
managing his part of the machinery as he is told to do. If, therefore,
I found myself in that compartment of a train designated by the

sovereign law of the state for presumable Caucasians, and for colored persons only when traveling in the capacity of nurses and maids, should a conductor inform me, as a gentleman might, that I had made a mistake, and offer to show me the proper car for black ladies; I might wonder at the expensive arrangements of the company and of the state in providing special and separate accommodations for the transportation of the various hues of humanity, but I certainly could not take it as a want of courtesy on the conductor's part that he gave the information. It is true, public sentiment precedes and begets all laws, good or bad; and on the ground I have taken, our women are to be credited largely as teachers and moulders of public sentiment. But when a law has passed and received the sanction of the land, there is nothing for our officials to do but enforce it till repealed; and I for one, as a loyal American citizen, will give those officials cheerful support and ready sympathy in the discharge of their duty. But when a great burly six feet of masculinity with sloping shoulders and unkempt beard swaggers in, and, throwing a roll of tobacco into one corner of his jaw, growls out at me over the paper I am reading, "Here gurl," (I am past thirty) "you better git out 'n dis kyar 'f yer don't, I'll put yer out,"—my mental annotation is *Here's an American citizen who has been badly trained. He is sadly lacking in both 'sweetness' and 'light'*; and when in the same section of our enlightened and progressive country, I see from the car window, working on private estates, convicts from the state penitentiary, among them squads of boys from fourteen to eighteen years of age in a chain-gang, their feet chained together and heavy blocks attached—not in 1850, but in 1890, '91 and '92, I make a note on the flyleaf of my memorandum, *The women in this section should organize a Society for the Prevention of Cruelty to Human Beings, and disseminate civilizing tracts, and send throughout the region apostles of anti-barbarism for the propagation of humane and enlightened ideas*. And when farther on in the same section our train stops at a dilapidated station, rendered yet more unsightly by dozens of loafers with their hands in their pockets while a productive soil and inviting climate beckon in vain to industry; and when, looking a little more closely, I see two dingy little rooms with "FOR LADIES" swinging over one and "FOR COLORED PEOPLE" over the other; while wondering under which head I come, I notice a little way off the only hotel proprietor of the place whittling a pine stick as he sits with one leg thrown across an empty goods box; and as my eye falls on a sample room next door which seems to be driving the only wide-awake and popular business of the commonwealth, I cannot help ejaculating under my breath, "What a field for the missionary woman." I know that if by any fatality I should be obliged to lie over at that station, and, driven by hunger, should be compelled to seek refreshments or the bare necessaries of life at the only public accommodation in the town, that same stick-whittler would coolly inform me, without looking up from his pine splinter, "We doan uccommodate no niggers hyur." And yet we are so scandalized at Russia's barbarity and cruelty to the Jews! We pay a man a thousand dollars a night just to make us weep, by a recital of such heathenish inhumanity as is practiced on Slavonic soil.

A recent writer on Eastern nations says: "If we take through the earth's temperate zone, a belt of country whose northern and southern edges are determined by certain limiting isotherms, not more than half the width of the zone apart, we shall find that we have included in a relatively small extent of surface almost all the nations of note in the world, past or present. Now, if we examine this belt and compare the different parts of it with one another, we shall be struck by a remarkable fact. *The peoples inhabiting it grow steadily more personal as we go west.* So unmistakable is this gradation, that one is almost tempted to ascribe it to cosmical rather than to human causes. It is as marked as the change in color of the human complexion observable along any meridian, which ranges from black at the equator to blonde toward the pole. In like manner the sense of self grows more intense as we follow in the wake of the setting sun, and fades steadily as we advance into the dawn. America, Europe, the Levant, India, Japan, each is less personal than the one before. . . . . *That politeness should be one of the most marked results of impersonality* may appear surprising, yet a slight examination will show it to be a fact. Considered *a priori*, the connection is not far to seek. Impersonality by lessening the interest in one's self, induces one to take an interest in others. Looked at *a posteriori*, we find that where the one trait exists the other is most developed, while an absence of the second seems to prevent the full growth of the first. This is true both in general and in detail. *Courtesy increases as we travel eastward round, the world, coincidently with a decrease in the sense of self,* Asia is more courteous than Europe, Europe than America. Particular races show the same concomitance of characteristics. France, the most impersonal nation of Europe, is at the same time the most polite."

And by inference, Americans, the most personal, are the least courteous nation on the globe.

The Black Woman had reached this same conclusion by an entirely different route; but it is gratifying to vanity, nevertheless, to find one's self sustained by both science and philosophy in a conviction, wrought in by hard experience, and yet too apparently audacious to be entertained even as a stealthy surmise. In fact the Black Woman was emboldened some time since by a well put and timely article from an Editor's Drawer on the "Mannerless Sex," to give the world the benefit of some of her experience with the "*Mannerless Race*"; but since Mr. Lowell shows so conclusively that the entire Land of the West is a *mannerless continent*, I have determined to plead with our women, the mannerless sex on this mannerless continent, to institute a reform by placing immediately in our national curricula a department for teaching GOOD MANNERS.

Now, am I right in holding the American Woman responsible? Is it true that the exponents of woman's advancement, the leaders in woman's thought, the preachers and teachers of all woman's reforms, can teach this nation to be courteous, to be pitiful, having compassion one of another, not rendering evil for inoffensiveness, and railing in proportion to the improbability of being struck back; but contrariwise, being *all* of one mind, to love as brethren?

I think so.

It may require some heroic measures, and like all revolutions will call for a determined front and a courageous, unwavering, stalwart heart on the part of the leaders of the reform.

The "*all*" will inevitably stick in the throat of the Southern woman. She must be allowed, please, to except the 'darkey' from the 'all'; it is too bitter a pill with black people in it. You must get the Revised Version to put it, "*love all white people* as brethren." She really could not enter any society on earth, or in heaven above, or in—the waters under the earth, on such unpalatable conditions.

The Black Woman has tried to understand the Southern woman's difficulties; to put herself in her place, and to be as fair, as charitable, and as free from prejudice in judging her antipathies, as she would have others in regard to her own. She has honestly weighed the apparently sincere excuse, "But you must remember that these people were once our slaves"; and that other, "But civility towards the Negroes will bring us on *social equality* with them."

These are the two bugbears; or rather, the two humbugbears: for, though each is founded on a most glaring fallacy, one would think they were words to conjure with, so potent and irresistible is their spell as an argument at the North as well as in the South.

One of the most singular facts about the unwritten history of this country is the consummate ability with which Southern influence, Southern ideas and Southern ideals, have from the very beginning even up to the present day, dictated to and domineered over the brain and sinew of this nation. Without wealth, without education, without inventions, arts, sciences, or industries, without well-nigh every one of the progressive ideas and impulses which have made this country great, prosperous and happy, personally indolent and practically stupid, poor in everything but bluster and self-esteem, the Southerner has nevertheless with Italian finesse and exquisite skill, uniformly and invariably, so manipulated Northern sentiment as to succeed sooner or later in carrying his point and shaping the policy of this government to suit his purposes. Indeed, the Southerner is a magnificent manager of men, a born educator. For two hundred and fifty years he trained to his hand a people whom he made absolutely his own, in body, mind, and sensibility. He so insinuated differences and distinctions among them, that their personal attachment for him was stronger than for their own brethren and fellow sufferers. He made it a crime for two or three of them to be gathered together in Christ's name without a white man's supervision, and a felony for one to teach them to read even the Word of Life; and yet they would defend his interest with their life blood; his smile was their happiness, a pat on the shoulder from him their reward. The slightest difference among themselves in condition, circumstances, opportunities, became barriers of jealousy and disunion. He sowed his blood broadcast among them, then pitted mulatto against black, bond against free, house slave against plantation slave, even the slave of one clan against like slave of another clan; till, wholly oblivious of their ability for mutual succor and defense, all became centers of myriad systems of repellent forces, having but one sentiment in common, and that their entire subjection to that master hand.

And he not only managed the black man, he also hoodwinked the white man, the tourist and investigator who visited his lordly estates. The slaves were doing well, in fact couldn't be happier,—plenty to eat, plenty to drink, comfortably housed and clothed—they

wouldn't be free if they could; in short, in his broad brimmed plantation hat and easy aristocratic smoking gown, he made you think
him a veritable patriarch in the midst of a lazy, well fed, good
natured, over-indulged tenantry.

Then, too, the South represented blood—not red blood, but
blue blood. The difference is in the length of the stream and your
distance from its source. If your own father was a pirate, a robber,
a murderer, his hands are dyed in red blood, and you don't say very
much about it. But if your great great great grandfather's grandfather stole and pillaged and slew, and you can prove it, your blood
has become blue and you are at great pains to establish the relationship. So the South had neither silver nor gold, but she had blood;
and she paraded it with so much gusto that the substantial little
Puritan maidens of the North, who had been making bread and
canning currants and not thinking of blood the least bit, began to
hunt up the records of the Mayflower to see if some of the passengers thereon could not claim the honor of having been one of
William the Conqueror's brigands, when he killed the last of the
Saxon kings and, red-handed, stole his crown and his lands. Thus
the ideal from out the Southland brooded over the nation and we
sing less lustily than of yore

> 'Kind hearts are more than coronets
> And simple faith than Norman blood.'

In politics, the two great forces, commerce and empire, which
would otherwise have shaped the destiny of the country, have been
made to pander and cater to Southern notions. "Cotton is King"
meant the South must be allowed to dictate or there would be no
fun. Every statesman from 1830 to 1860 exhausted his genius in
persuasion and compromises to smooth out her ruffled temper and
gratify her petulant demands. But like a sullen younger sister, the
South has pouted and sulked and cried: "I won't play with you
now; so there!" and the big brother at the North has coaxed and
compromised and given in, and—ended by letting her have her
way. Until 1860 she had as her pet an institution which it was death
by the law to say anything about, except that it was divinely insti-
tuted, inaugurated by Noah, sanctioned by Abraham, approved by
Paul, and just ideally perfect in every way. And when, to preserve
the autonomy of the family arrangements, in '61, '62 and '63, it

became necessary for the big brother to administer a little whole-some correction and set the obstreperous Miss vigorously down in her seat again, she assumed such an air of injured innocence, and melted away so lugubriously, the big brother has done nothing since but try to sweeten and pacify and laugh her back into a com-panionable frame of mind.

Father Lincoln did all he could to get her to repent of her petu-lance and behave herself. He even promised she might keep her pet, so disagreeable to all the neighbors and hurtful even to herself, and might manage it at home to suit herself, if she would only listen to reason and be just tolerably nice. But, no—she was going to leave and set up for herself; she didn't propose to be meddled with; and so, of course, she had to be spanked. Just a little at first—didn't mean to hurt, merely to teach her who was who. But she grew so ugly, and kicked and fought and scratched so outrageously, and seemed so determined to smash up the whole business, the head of the family got red in the face, and said: "Well, now, he couldn't have any more of that foolishness. Arabella must just behave herself or take the consequences." And after the spanking, Arabella sniffed and whimpered and pouted, and the big brother bit his lip, looked half ashamed, and said: "Well, I didn't want to hurt you. You needn't feel so awfully bad about it, I only did it for your good. You know I wouldn't do anything to displease you if I could help it; but you would insist on making the row, and so I just had to. Now, there—there—let's be friends!" and he put his great strong arms about her and just dared anybody to refer to that little unpleas-antness—he'd show them a thing or two. Still Arabella sulked,—till the rest of the family decided she might just keep her pets, and manage her own affairs and nobody should interfere.

So now, if one intimates that some clauses of the Constitution are a dead letter at the South and that only the name and support of that pet institution are changed while the fact and essence, minus the expense and responsibility, remain, he is quickly told to mind his own business and informed that he is waving the bloody shirt.

Even twenty-five years after the fourteenth and fifteenth amend-ments to our Constitution, a man who has been most unequivocal in his outspoken condemnation of the wrongs regularly and system-atically heaped on the oppressed race in this country, and on all even most remotely connected with them—a man whom we had thought our staunchest friend and most noble champion and defender—after a two weeks' trip in Georgia and Florida immediately gives signs of the fatal inception of the virus. Not even the chance traveller from England or Scotland escapes. The arch-manipulator takes him under his special watch-care and training, uses up his stock arguments and gives object lessons with his choicest specimens of Negro depravity and worthlessness; takes him through what, in New York, would be called "the slums," and would predicate there nothing but the duty of enlightened Christians to send out their light and emulate their Master's aggressive labors of love; but in Georgia is denominated "our terrible problem, which people of the North so little understand, yet vouchsafe so much gratuitous advice about." With an injured air he shows the stupendous and atrocious mistake of reasoning about these people as if they were just ordinary human beings, and amenable to the tenets of the Gospel; and not long after the inoculation begins to work, you hear this old-time friend of the oppressed delivering himself something after this fashion: "Ah, well, the South must be left to manage the Negro. She is most directly concerned and must understand her problem better than outsiders. We must not meddle. We must be very careful not to widen the breaches. The Negro is not worth a feud between brothers and sisters."

Lately a great national and international movement characteristic of this age and country, a movement based on the inherent right of every soul to its own highest development, I mean the movement making for Woman's full, free, and complete emancipation, has, after much courting, obtained the gracious smile of the Southern woman—I beg her pardon—the Southern *lady*.

She represents blood, and of course could not be expected to leave that out; and firstly and foremostly she must not, in any organization she may deign to grace with her presence, be asked to associate with "these people who were once her slaves."

Now the Southern woman (I may be pardoned, being one myself) was never renowned for her reasoning powers, and it is not surprising that just a little picking will make her logic fall to pieces even here.

In the first place she imagines that because her grandfather had slaves who were black, all the blacks in the world of every shade and tint were once in the position of her slaves. This is as bad as the

Irishman who was about to kill a peaceable Jew in the streets of
Cork,—having just learned that Jews slew his Redeemer. The black
race constitutes one-seventh the known population of the globe;
and there are representatives of it here as elsewhere who were never
in bondage at any time to any man,—whose blood is as blue and
lineage as noble as any, even that of the white lady of the South.
That her slaves were black and she despises her slaves, should no
more argue antipathy to all dark people and peoples, than that
Guiteau, an assassin, was white, and I hate assassins, should make
me hate all persons more or less white. The objection shows a want
of clear discrimination.

The second fallacy in the objection grows out of the use of an
ambiguous middle, as the logicians would call it, or assigning a
double signification to the term "*Social equality.*"

Civility to the Negro implies social equality. I am opposed to
associating with dark persons on terms of social equality. Therefore,
I abrogate civility to the Negro. This is like

> Light is opposed to darkness.
> Feathers are light.
> *Ergo,* Feathers are opposed to darkness.

The "social equality" implied by civility to the Negro is a very
different thing from forced, association with him socially. Indeed it
seems to me that the mere application of a little cold common sense
would show that uncongenial social environments could by no
means be forced on any one. I do not, and cannot be made to
associate with all dark persons, simply on the ground that I am dark;
and I presume the Southern lady can imagine some whose faces are
white, with whom she would no sooner think of chatting unreserv-
edly than, were it possible, with a veritable 'darkey.' Such things
must and will always be left to individual election. No law, human
or divine, can legislate for or against them. Like seeks like; and I am
sure with the Southern lady's antipathies at their present tempera-
ture, she might enter ten thousand organizations besprinkled with
colored women without being any more deflected by them than by
the proximity of a stone. The social equality scare then is all hum-
bug, conscious or unconscious, I know not which. And were it not
too bitter a thought to utter here, I might add that the overtures for
forced association in the past history of these two races were not

made by the manacled black man, nor by *the silent and suffering black woman!*

When I seek food in a public café or apply for first-class accommodations on a railway train, I do so because my physical necessities are identical with those of other human beings of like constitution and temperament, and crave satisfaction. I go because I want food, or I want comfort—not because I want association with those who frequent these places; and I can see no more "social equality" in buying lunch at the same restaurant, or riding in a common car, than there is in paying for dry goods at the same counter or walking on the same street.

The social equality which means forced or unbidden association would be as much deprecated and as strenuously opposed by the circle in which I move as by the most hide-bound Southerner in the land. Indeed I have been more than once annoyed by the inquisitive white interviewer, who, with spectacles on nose and pencil and note-book in hand, comes to get some "points" about "*your people.*" My "people" are just like other people—indeed, too like for their own good. They hate, they love, they attract and repel, they climb or they grovel, struggle or drift, aspire or despair, endure in hope or curse in vexation, exactly like all the rest of unregenerate humanity. Their likes and dislikes are as strong; their antipathies—and prejudices too I fear, are as pronounced as you will find anywhere; and the entrance to the inner sanctuary of their homes and hearts is as jealously guarded against profane intrusion.

What the dark man wants then is merely to live his own life, in his own world, with his own chosen companions, in whatever of comfort, luxury, or emoluments his talent or his money can in an impartial market secure. Has he wealth, he does not want to be forced into inconvenient or unsanitary sections of cities to buy a home and rear his family. Has he art, he does not want to be cabined and cribbed into emulation with the few who merely happen to have his complexion. His talent aspires to study without proscription the masters of all ages and to rub against the broadest and fullest movements of his own day.

Has he religion, he does not want to be made to feel that there is a white Christ and a black Christ, a white Heaven and a black Heaven, a white Gospel and a black Gospel,—but the one ideal of perfect manhood and womanhood, the one universal longing for development and growth, the one desire for being, and being better, the one great yearning, aspiring, outreaching, in all the heartthrobs of humanity in whatever race or clime.

A recent episode in the Corcoran art gallery at the American capital is to the point. A colored woman who had shown marked ability in drawing and coloring, was advised by her teacher, himself an artist of no mean rank, to apply for admission to the Corcoran school in order to study the models and to secure other advantages connected with the organization. She accordingly sent a written application accompanied by specimens of her drawings, the usual *modus operandi* in securing admission.

The drawings were examined by the best critics and pronounced excellent, and a ticket of admission was immediately issued together with a highly complimentary reference to her work.

The next day my friend, congratulating her country and herself that at least in the republic of art no caste existed, presented her ticket of admission *in propria persona*. There was a little preliminary side play in Delsarte pantomine,—aghast—incredulity—wonder; then the superintendent told her in plain unartistic English that of course he had not dreamed a colored person could do such work, and had he suspected the truth he would never have issued the ticket of admission; that, to be right frank, the ticket would have to be cancelled,—she could under no condition be admitted to the studio.

Can it be possible that even art in America is to be tainted by this shrivelling caste spirit? If so, what are we coming to? Can any one conceive a Shakespeare, a Michael Angelo, or a Beethoven putting away any fact of simple merit because the thought, or the suggestion, or the creation emanated from a soul with an unpleasing exterior?

What is it that makes the great English bard pre-eminent as the photographer of the human soul? Where did he learn the universal language, so that Parthians, Medes and Elamites, and the dwellers in Mesopotamia, in Egypt and Libya, in Crete and Arabia do hear every one in our own tongue the wonderful revelations of this myriad mind? How did he learn our language? Is it not that his own soul was infinitely receptive to Nature, the dear old nurse, in all her protean forms? Did he not catch and reveal her own secret by his sympathetic listening as she "would constantly sing a more wonderful song or tell a more marvellous tale" in the souls he met around him?

"Stand off! I am better than thou!" has never yet painted a true picture, nor written a thrilling song, nor given a pulsing, a soul-burning sermon. 'Tis only sympathy, another name for love,—that one poor word which, as George Eliot says, "expresses so much of human insight"—that can interpret either man or matter.

It was Shakespeare's own all-embracing sympathy, that infinite receptivity of his, and native, all-comprehending appreciation, which proved a key to unlock and open every soul that came within his radius. And *he received as much as he gave*. His own stores were infinitely enriched thereby. For it is decreed

> Man like the vine supported lives,
> The strength he gains is from th' embrace he gives.

It is only through clearing the eyes from bias and prejudice, and becoming one with the great all pervading soul of the universe that either art or science can

> "Read what is still unread
> In the manuscripts of God."

No true artist can allow himself to be narrowed and provincialized by deliberately shutting out any class of facts or subjects through prejudice against externals. And American art, American science, American literature can never be founded in truth, the universal beauty; can never learn to speak a language intelligible in all climes and for all ages, till this paralyzing grip of caste prejudice is loosened from its vitals, and the healthy sympathetic eye is taught to look out on the great universe as holding no favorites and no black beasts, but bearing in each plainest or loveliest feature the handwriting of its God.

And this is why, as it appears to me, woman in her lately acquired vantage ground for speaking an earnest helpful word, can do this country no deeper and truer and more lasting good than by bending all her energies to thus broadening, humanizing, and civilizing her native land.

"Except ye become as little children" is not a pious precept, but an inexorable law of the universe. God's kingdoms are all sealed to the seedy, moss-grown mind of self-satisfied maturity. Only the little child in spirit, the simple, receptive, educable mind can enter.

Preconceived notions, blinding prejudices, and shrivelling antipathies must be wiped out, and the cultivable soul made a *tabula rasa* for whatever lesson great Nature has to teach.

This, too, is why I conceive the subject to have been unfortunately worded which was chosen by Miss Shaw at the Woman's Council and which stands at the head of this chapter.

Miss Shaw is one of the most powerful of our leaders, and we feel her voice should give no uncertain note. Woman should not, even by inference, or for the sake of argument, seem to disparage what is weak. For woman's cause is the cause of the weak; and when all the weak shall have received their due consideration, then woman will have her "rights," and the Indian will have his rights, and the Negro will have his rights, and all the strong will have learned at last to deal justly, to love mercy, and to walk humbly; and our fair land will have been taught the secret of universal courtesy which is after all nothing but the art, the science, and the religion of regarding one's neighbor as one's self, and to do for him as we would, were conditions swapped, that he do for us.

It cannot seem less than a blunder, whenever the exponents of a great reform or the harbingers of a noble advance in thought and effort allow themselves to seem distorted by a narrow view of their own aims and principles. All prejudices, whether of race, sect or sex, class pride and caste distinctions are the belittling inheritance and badge of snobs and prigs.

The philosophic mind sees that its own "rights" are the rights of humanity. That in the universe of God nothing trivial is or mean; and the recognition it seeks is not through the robber and wild beast adjustment of the survival of the bullies but through the universal application ultimately of the Golden Rule.

Not unfrequently has it happened that the impetus of a mighty thought wave has done the execution meant by its Creator in spite of the weak and distorted perception of its human embodiment. It is not strange if reformers, who, after all, but think God's thoughts after him, have often "builded more wisely than they knew;" and while fighting consciously for only a narrow gateway for themselves, have been driven forward by that irresistible "Power not ourselves which makes for righteousness" to open a high road for humanity. It was so with our sixteenth century reformers. The fathers of the Reformation had no idea that they were inciting an insurrection of the human mind against all domination. None would have been more shocked than they at our nineteenth century deductions from their sixteenth century premises. Emancipation of mind and freedom of thought would have been as appalling to them as it was distasteful to the pope. They were right, they argued, to rebel against Romish absolutism—because Romish preaching and Romish practicing were wrong. They denounced popes for hacking heretics and forthwith began themselves to roast witches. The Spanish Inquisition in the hands of Philip and Alva was an institution of the devil; wielded by the faithful, it would become quite another thing. The only "rights" they were broad enough consciously to fight for was the right to substitute the absolutism of their conceptions, their party, their '*ism*' for an authority whose teaching they conceived to be corrupt and vicious. Persecution for a belief was wrong only when the persecutors were wrong and the persecuted right. The sacred prerogative of the individual to decide on matters of belief they did not dream of maintaining. Universal tolerance and its twin, universal charity, were not conceived yet. The broad foundation stone of all human rights, the great democratic principle "A man's a man, *and his own sovereign* for a' that" they did not dare enunciate. They were incapable of drawing up a Declaration of Independence for humanity. The Reformation to the Reformers meant one bundle of authoritative opinions vs. another bundle of authoritative opinions. Justification by faith, vs. justification by ritual. Submission to Calvin vs. submission to the Pope. English and Germans vs. the Italians.

To our eye, viewed through a vista of three centuries, it was the death wrestle of the principle of thought enslavement in the throttling grasp of personal freedom; it was the great Emancipation Day of human belief, man's intellectual Independence Day, prefiguring and finally compelling the world-wide enfranchisement of his body and all its activities. Not Protestant vs. Catholic, then; not Luther vs. Leo, not Dominicans vs. Augustinians, nor Geneva vs. Rome;— but humanity rationally free, vs. the clamps of tradition and superstition which had manacled and muzzled it.

The cause of freedom is not the cause of a race or a sect, a party or a class,—it is the cause of human kind, the very birthright of humanity. Now unless we are greatly mistaken the Reform of our day, known as the Woman's Movement, is essentially such an embodiment, if its pioneers could only realize it, of the universal good. And specially important is it that there be no confusion of ideas among its leaders as to its scope and universality. All mists must be cleared from the eyes of woman if she is to be a teacher of morals and manners: the former strikes its roots in the individual and its training and pruning may be accomplished by classes; but the latter is to lubricate the joints and minimize the friction of society, and it is important and fundamental that there be no chromatic or other aberration when the teacher is settling the point, "Who is my neighbor?"

It is not the intelligent woman vs. the ignorant woman; nor the white woman vs. the black, the brown, and the red,—it is not even the cause of woman vs. man. Nay, 'tis woman's strongest vindication for speaking that *the world needs to hear her voice*. It would be subversive of every human interest that the cry of one-half the human family be stifled. Woman in stepping from the pedestal of statue-like inactivity in the domestic shrine, and daring to think and move and speak,—to undertake to help shape, mold, and direct the thought of her age, is merely completing the circle of the world's vision. Hers is every interest that has lacked an interpreter and a defender. Her cause is linked with that of every agony that has been dumb—every wrong that needs a voice.

It is no fault of man's that he has not been able to see truth from her standpoint. It does credit both to his head and heart that no greater mistakes have been committed or even wrongs perpetrated while she sat making tatting and snipping paper flowers. Man's own innate chivalry and the mutual interdependence of their interests have insured his treating her cause, in the main at least, as his own. And he is pardonably surprised and even a little chagrined, perhaps, to find his legislation not considered "perfectly lovely" in every respect. But in any case his work is only impoverished by her remaining dumb. The world has had to limp along with the wobbling gait and one-sided hesitancy of a man with one eye. Suddenly the bandage is removed from the other eye and the whole body is filled with light. It sees a circle where before it saw a segment. The darkened eye restored, every member rejoices with it.

What a travesty of its case for this eye to become plaintiff in a suit, *Eye vs. Foot*. "There is that dull clod, the foot, allowed to roam at will, free and untrammelled; while I, the source and medium of light, brilliant and beautiful, am fettered in darkness and doomed to desuetude." The great burly black man, ignorant and gross and depraved, is allowed to vote; while the franchise is withheld from the intelligent and refined, the pure-minded and lofty souled white woman. Even the untamed and untamable Indian of the prairie, who can answer nothing but 'ugh' to great economic and civic questions is thought by some worthy to wield the ballot which is still denied the Puritan maid and the first lady of Virginia.

Is not this hitching our wagon to something much lower than a star? Is not woman's cause broader, and deeper, and grander, than a blue stocking debate or an aristocratic pink tea? Why should woman become plaintiff in a suit versus the Indian, or the Negro or any other race or class who have been crushed under the iron heel of Anglo-Saxon power and selfishness? If the Indian has been wronged and cheated by the puissance of this American government, it is woman's mission to plead with her country to cease to do evil and to pay its honest debts. If the Negro has been deceitfully cajoled or inhumanly cuffed according to selfish expediency or capricious antipathy, let it be woman's mission to plead that he be met as a man and honestly given half the road. If woman's own happiness has been ignored or misunderstood in our country's legislating for bread winners, for rum sellers, for property holders, for the family relations, for any or all the interests that touch her vitally, let her rest her plea, not on Indian inferiority, nor on Negro depravity, but on the obligation of legislators to do for her as they would have others do for them were relations reversed. Let her try to teach her country that every interest in this world is entitled at least to a respectful hearing, that every sentiency is worthy of its own gratification, that a helpless cause should not be trampled down, nor a bruised reed broken; and when the right of the individual is made sacred, when the image of God in human form, whether in marble or in clay, whether in alabaster or in ebony, is consecrated and inviolable, when men have been taught to look beneath the rags and grime, the pomp and pageantry of mere circumstance and have regard unto the celestial kernel uncontaminated at the core,—when race, color, sex, condition, are realized to be the accidents, not the substance of life, and consequently as not obscuring or modifying the inalienable title to life, liberty, and pursuit of happiness,—then is mastered the science of politeness, the art of courteous contact, which is naught but the practical application of the principle of benevolence, the back bone and marrow of all religion; then woman's lesson is taught and woman's cause is won—not the white woman nor the black woman nor the red

woman, but the cause of every man or woman who has writhed
silently under a mighty wrong. The pleading of the American
woman for the right and the opportunity to employ the American
method of influencing the disposal to be made of herself, her property, her children in civil, economic, or domestic relations is thus
seen to be based on a principle as broad as the human race and as
old as human society. Her wrongs are thus indissolubly linked with
all undefended woe, all helpless suffering, and the plenitude of her
"rights" will mean the final triumph of all right over might, the
supremacy of the moral forces of reason and justice and love in the
government of the nation.

God hasten the day.

THE STATUS OF WOMAN IN AMERICA

JUST FOUR HUNDRED years ago an obscure dreamer and castle builder, prosaically poor and ridiculously insistent on the reality of his dreams, was enabled through the devotion of a noble woman to give to civilization a magnificent continent.

What the lofty purpose of Spain's pure-minded queen had brought to the birth, the untiring devotion of pioneer women nourished and developed. The dangers of wild beasts and of wilder men, the mysteries of unknown wastes and unexplored forests, the horrors of pestilence and famine, of exposure and loneliness, during all those years of discovery and settlement, were braved without a murmur by women who had been most delicately constituted and most tenderly nurtured.

And when the times of physical hardship and danger were past, when the work of clearing and opening up was over and the struggle for accumulation began, again woman's inspiration and help were needed and still was she loyally at hand. A Mary Lyon, demanding and making possible equal advantages of education for women as for men, and, in the face of discouragement and incredulity, bequeathing to women the opportunities of Holyoke.

A Dorothea Dix, insisting on the humane and rational treatment of the insane and bringing about a reform in the lunatic asylums of the country, making a great step forward in the tender regard for the weak by the strong throughout the world.

A Helen Hunt Jackson, convicting the nation of a century of dishonor in regard to the Indian.

A Lucretia Mott, gentle Quaker spirit, with sweet insistence, preaching the abolition of slavery and the institution, in its stead, of the brotherhood of man; her life and words breathing out in tender melody the injunction

"Have love. Not love alone for one
But man as man thy brother call;
And scatter, like the circling sun,
Thy charities *on all*."

And at the most trying time of what we have called the Accumulative
Period, when internecine war, originated through man's love of
gain and his determination to subordinate national interests and
black men's rights alike to considerations of personal profit and loss,
was drenching our country with its own best blood, who shall
recount the name and fame of the women on both sides the senseless
strife,—those uncomplaining souls with a great heart ache of their
own, rigid features and pallid cheek their ever effective flag of truce,
on the battle field, in the camp, in the hospital, binding up wounds,
recording dying whispers for absent loved ones, with tearful eyes
pointing to man's last refuge, giving the last earthly hand clasp and
performing the last friendly office for strangers whom a great common sorrow had made kin, while they knew that somewhere—
somewhere a husband, a brother, a father, a son, was being tended
by stranger hands—or mayhap those familiar eyes were even then
being closed forever by just such another ministering angel of mercy
and love.

But why mention names? Time would fail to tell of the noble
army of women who shine like beacon lights in the otherwise sordid wilderness of this accumulative period—prison reformers and
tenement cleansers, quiet unnoted workers in hospitals and homes,
among imbeciles, among outcasts—the sweetening, purifying anti-
dotes for the poisons of man's acquisitiveness,—mollifying and
soothing with the tenderness of compassion and love the wounds
and bruises caused by his overreaching and avarice.

The desire for quick returns and large profits tempts capital ofttimes into unsanitary, well nigh inhuman investments,—tenement
tinder boxes, stifling, stunting, sickening alleys and pestiferous
slums; regular rents, no waiting, large percentages,—rich coffers
coined out of the life-blood of human bodies and souls. Men and
women herded together like cattle, breathing in malaria and typhus
from an atmosphere seething with moral as well as physical impu-
rity, revelling in vice as their native habitat and then, to drown the
whisperings of their higher consciousness and effectually to hush
the yearnings and accusations within, flying to narcotics and

opiates—rum, tobacco, opium, binding hand and foot, body and soul, till the proper image of God is transformed into a fit associate for demons,—a besotted, enervated, idiotic wreck, or else a monster of wickedness terrible and destructive.

These are some of the legitimate products of the unmitigated tendencies of the wealth-producing period. But, thank Heaven, side by side with the cold, mathematical, selfishly calculating, so-called practical and unsentimental instinct of the business man, there comes the sympathetic warmth and sunshine of good women, like the sweet and sweetening breezes of spring, cleansing, purifying, soothing, inspiring, lifting the drunkard from the gutter, the outcast from the pit. Who can estimate the influence of these "daughters of the king," these lend-a-hand forces, in counteracting the selfishness of an acquisitive age?

To-day America counts her millionaires by the thousand; questions of tariff and questions of currency are the most vital ones agitating the public mind. In this period, when material prosperity and well earned ease and luxury are assured facts from a national standpoint, woman's work and woman's influence are needed as never before; needed to bring a heart power into this money getting, dollar-worshipping civilization; needed to bring a moral force into the utilitarian motives and interests of the time; needed to stand for God and Home and Native Land *versus gain and greed and grasping selfishness.*

There can be no doubt that this fourth centenary of America's discovery which we celebrate at Chicago, strikes the keynote of another important transition in the history of this nation; and the prominence of woman in the management of its celebration is a fitting tribute to the part she is destined to play among the forces of the future. This is the first congressional recognition of woman in this country, and this Board of Lady Managers constitute the first women legally appointed by any government to act in a national capacity. This of itself marks the dawn of a new day.

Now the periods of discovery, of settlement, of developing resources and accumulating wealth have passed in rapid succession. Wealth in the nation as in the individual brings leisure, repose, reflection. The struggle with nature is over, the struggle with ideas begins. We stand then, it seems to me, in this last decade of the nineteenth century, just in the portals of a new and untried movement on a higher plain and in a grander strain than any the past has called forth. It does not require a prophet's eye to divine its trend and image its possibilities from the forces we see already at work around us; nor is it hard to guess what must be the status of woman's work under the new regime.

In the pioneer days her role was that of a camp-follower, an additional something to fight for and be burdened with, only repaying the anxiety and labor she called forth by her own incomparable gifts of sympathy and appreciative love; unable herself ordinarily to contend with the bear and the Indian, or to take active part in clearing the wilderness and constructing the home.

In the second or wealth producing period her work is abreast of man's, complementing and supplementing, counteracting excessive tendencies, and mollifying over rigorous proclivities.

In the era now about to dawn, her sentiments must strike the keynote and give the dominant tone. And this because of the nature of her contribution to the world.

Her kingdom is not over physical forces. Not by might, nor by power can she prevail. Her position must ever be inferior where strength of muscle creates leadership. If she follows the instincts of her nature, however, she must always stand for the conservation of those deeper moral forces which make for the happiness of homes and the righteousness of the country. In a reign of moral ideas she is easily queen.

There is to my mind no grander and surer prophecy of the new era and of woman's place in it, than the work already begun in the waning years of the nineteenth century by the W. C. T. U. in America, an organization which has even now reached not only national but international importance, and seems destined to permeate and purify the whole civilized world. It is the living embodiment of woman's activities and woman's ideas, and its extent and strength rightly prefigure her increasing power as a moral factor.

The colored woman of to-day occupies, one may say, a unique position in this country. In a period of itself transitional and unsettled, her status seems one of the least ascertainable and definitive of all the forces which make for our civilization. She is confronted by both a woman question and a race problem, and is as yet an unknown or an unacknowledged factor in both. While the women of the white race can with calm assurance enter upon the work they feel by nature appointed to do, while their men give loyal support and appreciative countenance to their efforts, recognizing in most avenues of usefulness the propriety and the need of woman's distinctive co-operation, the colored woman too often finds herself hampered and shamed by a less liberal sentiment and a more conservative attitude on the part of those for whose opinion she cares most. That this is not universally true I am glad to admit. There are to be found both intensely conservative white men and exceedingly liberal colored men. But as far as my experience goes the average man of our race is less frequently ready to admit the actual need among the sturdier forces of the world for woman's help or influence. That great social and economic questions await her interference, that she could throw any light on problems of national import, that her intermeddling could improve the management of school systems, or elevate the tone of public institutions, or humanize and sanctify the far reaching influence of prisons and reformatories and improve the treatment of lunatics and imbeciles,—that she has a word worth hearing on mooted questions in political economy, that she could contribute a suggestion on the relations of labor and capital, or offer a thought on honest money and honorable trade, I fear the majority of "Americans of the colored variety" are not yet prepared to concede. It may be that they do not yet see these questions in their right perspective, being absorbed in the immediate needs of their own political complications. A good deal depends on where we put the emphasis in this world; and our men are not perhaps to blame if they see everything colored by the light of those agitations in the midst of which they live and move and have their being. The part they have had to play in American history during the last twenty-five or thirty years has tended rather to exaggerate the importance of mere political advantage, as well as to set a fictitious valuation on those able to secure such advantage. It is the astute politician, the manager who can gain preferment for himself and his favorites, the demagogue known to stand in with the powers at the White House and consulted on the bestowal of government plums, whom we set in high places and denominate great. It is they who receive the hosannas of the multitude and are regarded as leaders of the people. The thinker and the doer, the man who solves the problem by enriching his country with an invention worth thousands or by a thought inestimable and precious is given neither bread nor a stone. He is too often left to die in obscurity and neglect even if spared in his life the bitterness of fanatical jealousies and detraction.

And yet politics, and surely American politics, is hardly a school for great minds. Sharpening rather than deepening, it develops the faculty of taking advantage of present emergencies rather than the insight to distinguish between the true and the false, the lasting and the ephemeral advantage. Highly cultivated selfishness rather than consecrated benevolence is its passport to success. Its votaries are never seers. At best they are but manipulators—often only jugglers. It is conducive neither to profound statesmanship nor to the higher type of manhood. Altruism is its *mauvais succes* and naturally enough it is indifferent to any factor which cannot be worked into its own immediate aims and purposes. As woman's influence as a political element is as yet nil in most of the commonwealths of our republic, it is not surprising that with those who place the emphasis on mere political capital she may yet seem almost a nonentity so far as it concerns the solution of great national or even racial perplexities.

There are those, however, who value the calm elevation of the thoughtful spectator who stands aloof from the heated scramble; and, above the turmoil and din of corruption and selfishness, can listen to the teachings of eternal truth and righteousness. There are even those who feel that the black man's unjust and unlawful exclusion temporarily from participation in the elective franchise in certain states is after all but a lesson "in the desert" fitted to develop in him insight and discrimination against the day of his own appointed time. One needs occasionally to stand aside from the hum and rush of human interests and passions to hear the voices of God. And it not unfrequently happens that the All-loving gives a great push to certain souls to thrust them out, as it were, from the distracting current for awhile to promote their discipline and growth, or to enrich them by communion and reflection. And similarly it may be woman's privilege from her peculiar coigne of vantage as a quiet observer, to whisper just the needed suggestion or the almost forgotten truth. The colored woman, then, should not be ignored because her bark is resting in the silent waters of the sheltered cove. She is watching the movements of the contestants none the less and is all the better qualified, perhaps, to weigh and judge and advise because not herself in the excitement of the race. Her voice, too, has always been heard in clear, unfaltering tones, ringing the changes on those deeper interests which make for permanent good. She is always sound and orthodox on questions affecting the well-being of her race. You do not find the colored woman selling her birthright for a mess of pottage. Nay, even after reason has retired from the contest, she has been known to cling blindly with the instinct of a turtle dove to those principles and policies which to her mind promise hope and safety for children yet unborn. It is notorious that ignorant black women in the South have actually left their husbands' homes and repudiated their support for what was understood by the wife to be race disloyalty, or "voting away," as she expresses it, the privileges of herself and little ones.

It is largely our women in the South to-day who keep the black men solid in the Republican party. The latter as they increase in intelligence and power of discrimination would be more apt to divide on local issues at any rate. They begin to see that the Grand Old Party regards the Negro's cause as an outgrown issue, and on Southern soil at least finds a too intimate acquaintanceship with him a somewhat unsavory recommendation. Then, too, their political wits have been sharpened to appreciate the fact that it is good policy to cultivate one's neighbors and not depend too much on a distant friend to fight one's home battles. But the black woman can never forget—however lukewarm the party may to-day appear—that it was a Republican president who struck the manacles from her own wrists and gave the possibilities of manhood to her helpless little ones; and to her mind a Democratic Negro is a traitor and a time-server. Talk as much as you like of venality and manipulation in the South, there are not many men, I can tell you, who would dare face a wife quivering in every fiber with the consciousness that her husband is a coward who could be paid to desert her deepest and dearest interests.

Not unfelt, then, if unproclaimed has been the work and influence of the colored women of America. Our list of chieftains in the service, though not long, is not inferior in strength and excellence, I dare believe, to any similar list which this country can produce.

Among the pioneers, Frances Watkins Harper could sing with prophetic exaltation in the darkest days, when as yet there was not a rift in the clouds overhanging her people:

> "Yes, Ethiopia shall stretch
> Her bleeding hands abroad;
> Her cry of agony shall reach the burning throne of God.

Redeemed from dust and freed from chains
　　Her sons shall lift their eyes,
From cloud-capt hills and verdant plains
　　Shall shouts of triumph rise."

Among preachers of righteousness, an unanswerable silencer of
cavilers and objectors, was Sojourner Truth, that unique and rugged genius who seemed carved out without hand or chisel from the
solid mountain mass; and in pleasing contrast, Amanda Smith,
sweetest of natural singers and pleaders in dulcet tones for the things
of God and of His Christ.

Sarah Woodson Early and Martha Briggs, planting and watering
in the school room, and giving off from their matchless and irresistible personality an impetus and inspiration which can never die so
long as there lives and breathes a remote descendant of their disci-
ples and friends.

Charlotte Fortin Grimke, the gentle spirit whose verses and life
link her so beautifully with America's great Quaker poet and loving
reformer.

Hallie Quinn Brown, charming reader, earnest, effective lecturer
and devoted worker of unflagging zeal and unquestioned power.

Fannie Jackson Coppin, the teacher and organizer, pre-eminent
among women of whatever country or race in constructive and
executive force.

These women represent all shades of belief and as many departments of activity; but they have one thing in common—their sympathy with the oppressed race in America and the consecration of
their several talents in whatever line to the work of its deliverance
and development.

Fifty years ago woman's activity according to orthodox defini-
tions was on a pretty clearly cut "sphere," including primarily the
kitchen and the nursery, and rescued from the barrenness of prison
bars by the womanly mania for adorning every discoverable bit of
china or canvass with forlorn looking cranes balanced idiotically on
one foot. The woman of to-day finds herself in the presence of
responsibilities which ramify through the profoundest and most
varied interests of her country and race. Not one of the issues of
this plodding, toiling, sinning, repenting, falling, aspiring humanity
can afford to shut her out, or can deny the reality of her influence.
No plan for renovating society, no scheme for purifying politics, no

reform in church or in state, no moral, social, or economic question, no movement upward or downward in the human plane is lost on her. A man once said when told his house was afire: "Go tell my wife; I never meddle with household affairs." But no woman can possibly put herself or her sex outside any of the interests that affect humanity. All departments in the new era are to be hers, in the sense that her interests are in all and through all; and it is incumbent on her to keep intelligently and sympathetically *en rapport* with all the great movements of her time, that she may know on which side to throw the weight of her influence. She stands now at the gateway of this new era of American civilization. In her hands must be moulded the strength, the wit, the statesmanship, the morality, all the psychic force, the social and economic intercourse of that era. To be alive at such an epoch is a privilege, to be a woman then is sublime.

In this last decade of our century, changes of such moment are in progress, such new and alluring vistas are opening out before us, such original and radical suggestions for the adjustment of labor and capital, of government and the governed, of the family, the church and the state, that to be a possible factor though an infinitesimal in such a movement is pregnant with hope and weighty with responsibility. To be a woman in such an age carries with it a privilege and an opportunity never implied before. But to be a woman of the Negro race in America, and to be able to grasp the deep significance of the possibilities of the crisis, is to have a heritage, it seems to me, unique in the ages. In the first place, the race is young and full of the elasticity and hopefulness of youth. All its achievements are before it. It does not look on the masterly triumphs of nineteenth century civilization with that *blasé* world-weary look which characterizes the old washed out and worn out races which have already, so to speak, seen their best days.

Said a European writer recently: "Except the Slavonic, the Negro is the only original and distinctive genius which has yet to come to growth—and the feeling is to cherish and develop it."

Everything to this race is new and strange and inspiring. There is a quickening of its pulses and a glowing of its self-consciousness. Aha, I can rival that! I can aspire to that! I can honor my name and vindicate my race! Something like this, it strikes me, is the enthusiasm which stirs the genius of young Africa in America; and the memory of past oppression and the fact of present attempted repression only serve to gather momentum for its irrepressible powers. Then again, a race in such a stage of growth is peculiarly sensitive to impressions. Not the photographer's sensitized plate is more delicately impressionable to outer influences than is this high strung people here on the threshold of a career.

What a responsibility then to have the sole management of the primal lights and shadows! Such is the colored woman's office. She must stamp weal or woe on the coming history of this people. May she see her opportunity and vindicate her high prerogative.

TUTTI AD LIBITUM

A *People* is but the attempt of many
To rise to the completer life of one.

   ★   ★   ★

The common *Problem*, yours, mine, every one's
Is—not to fancy what were fair in life
Provided it could be,—but, finding first
What may be, then find how to make it fair
Up to our means; a very different thing!
                    —*Robert Browning.*

   The greatest question in the world is how to give every man a man's share in what goes on in life—we want a freeman's share, and that is to think and speak and act about what concerns us all, and see whether these fine gentlemen who undertake to govern us are doing the best they can for us.—*Felix Holt.*

HAS AMERICA A RACE PROBLEM; IF SO, HOW CAN IT BEST BE SOLVED?

THERE ARE TWO kinds of peace in this world. The one produced by suppression, which is the passivity of death; the other brought about by a proper adjustment of living, acting forces. A nation or an individual may be at peace because all opponents have been killed or crushed; or, nation as well as individual may have found the secret of true harmony in the determination to live and let live.

A harmless looking man was once asked how many there were in his family.

"Ten," he replied grimly; "my wife's a one and I a zero." In that family there was harmony, to be sure, but it was the harmony of a despotism—it was the quiet of a muzzled mouth, the smoldering peace of a volcano crusted over.

Now I need not say that peace produced by suppression is neither natural nor desirable. Despotism is not one of the ideas that man has copied from nature. All through God's universe we see eternal harmony and symmetry as the unvarying result of the equilibrium of opposing forces. Fair play in an equal fight is the law written in Nature's book. And the solitary bully with his foot on the breast of his last antagonist has no warrant in any fact of God.

The beautiful curves described by planets and suns in their courses are the resultant of conflicting forces. Could the centrifugal force for one instant triumph, or should the centripetal grow weary and give up the struggle, immeasurable disaster would ensue—earth, moon, sun would go spinning off at a tangent or must fall helplessly into its master sphere. The acid counterbalances and keeps in order the alkali; the negative, the positive electrode. A proper equilibrium between a most inflammable explosive and the supporter of combustion, gives us water, the bland fluid that we cannot dispense with. Nay, the very air we breathe, which seems so calm, so peaceful, is rendered innocuous only by the constant conflict of opposing gases. Were the fiery, never-resting, all-corroding oxygen to gain the mastery we should be burnt to cinders in a trice. With the sluggish, inert nitrogen triumphant, we should die of inanition.

These facts are only a suggestion of what must be patent to every student of history. Progressive peace in a nation is the result of conflict; and conflict, such as is healthy, stimulating, and progressive, is produced through the co-existence of radically opposing or racially different elements. Bellamy's ox-like men pictured in *Looking Backward*, taking their daily modicum of provender from the grandmotherly government, with nothing to struggle for, no wrong to put down, no reform to push through, no rights to vindicate and uphold, are nice folks to read about; but they are not natural; they are not progressive. God's world is not governed that way. The child can never gain strength save by resistance, and there can be no resistance if all movement is in one direction and all opposition made forever an impossibility.

I confess I can see no deeper reason than this for the specializing of racial types in the world. Whatever our theory with reference to the origin of species and the unity of mankind, we cannot help admitting the fact that no sooner does a family of the human race take up its abode in some little nook between mountains, or on some plain walled in by their own hands, no sooner do they begin in earnest to live their own life, think their own thoughts, and trace out their own arts, than they begin also to crystallize some idea different from and generally opposed to that of other tribes or families.

Each race has its badge, its exponent, its message, branded in its forehead by the great Master's hand which is its own peculiar keynote, and its contribution to the harmony of nations.

Left entirely alone,—out of contact, that is with other races and their opposing ideas and conflicting tendencies, this cult is abnormally developed and there is unity without variety, a predominance of one tone at the expense of moderation and harmony, and finally a sameness, a monotonous dullness which means stagnation,—death.

It is this of which M. Guizot complains in Asiatic types of civilization; and in each case he mentions I note that there was but one race, one free force predominating.

In Lect. II. Hist. of Civ. he says:

"In Egypt the theocratic principle took possession of society and showed itself in its manners, its monuments and in all that has come down to us of Egyptian civilization. In India the same phenomenon occurs—a repetition of the almost exclusively prevailing influence of theocracy. In other regions the domination of a conquering caste; where such is the case the principle of force takes entire possession of society. In another place we discover society under the entire influence of the democratic principle. Such was the case in the commercial republics which covered the coasts of Asia Minor and Syria, in Ionia and Phœnicia. In a word whenever we contemplate the civilization of the ancients, we find them all impressed with *one ever prevailing character of unity*, visible in their institutions, their ideas and manners; *one sole influence seems to govern and determine all things*. . . . . In one nation, as in Greece, the unity of the social principle led to a development of wonderful rapidity; no other people ever ran so brilliant a career in so short a time. But Greece had hardly become glorious before she appeared worn out. Her decline was as sudden as her rise had been rapid. It seems as if the principle which called Greek civilization into life was exhausted. No other came to invigorate it or supply its place. In India and Egypt where again only one principle of civilization prevailed (*one race predominant you see*) society became stationary. Simplicity produced monotony. Society continued to exist, but there was no progression. It remained torpid and inactive.

Now I beg you to note that in none of these systems was a RACE PROBLEM possible. The dominant race had settled that matter forever. Asiatic society was fixed in cast iron molds. Virtually there was but one race inspiring and molding the thought, the art, the literature, the government. It was against this shrivelling caste prejudice and intolerance that the zealous Buddha set his face like a flint. And I do not think it was all blasphemy in Renan when he said Jesus Christ was first of democrats, i. e., a believer in the royalty of the individual, a preacher of the brotherhood of man through the fatherhood of God, a teacher who proved that the lines on which worlds are said to revolve are *imaginary*, that for all the distinctions of blue blood and black blood and red blood—*a man's a man for a' that*. Buddha and the Christ, each in his own way, wrought to rend asunder the clamps and bands of caste, and to thaw out the ice of race tyranny and exclusiveness. The Brahmin, who was Aryan, spurned a suggestion even, from the Sudra, who belonged to the hated and proscribed Turanian race. With a Pariah he could not eat or drink. They were to him outcasts and unclean. Association with them meant contamination; the hint of their social equality was blasphemous. Respectful consideration for their rights and feelings was almost a physical no less than a moral impossibility.

No more could the Helots among the Greeks have been said to contribute anything to the movement of their times. The dominant race had them effectually under its heel. It was the tyranny and exclusiveness of these nations, therefore, which brought about their immobility and resulted finally in the barrenness of their one idea. From this came the poverty and decay underlying their civilization, from this the transitory, ephemeral character of its brilliancy.

To quote Guizot again: "Society belonged to *one exclusive* power which could bear with no other. Every principle of a different tendency was proscribed. The governing principle would nowhere suffer by its side the manifestation and influence of a rival principle. This character of unity in their civilization is equally impressed upon their literature and intellectual productions. Those monuments of Hindoo literature lately introduced into Europe seem all struck from the same die. They all seem the result of one same fact, the expression of one idea. Religious and moral treatises, historical traditions, dramatic poetry, epics, all bear the same physiognomy. The same character of unity and monotony shines out in these works of mind and fancy, as we discover in their life and institutions." Not even Greece with all its classic treasures is made an exception from these limitations produced by exclusivness.

But the course of empire moves one degree westward. Europe becomes the theater of the leading exponents of civilization, and here we have a *Race Problem*,—if, indeed, the confused jumble of races, the clash and conflict, the din and devastation of those stormy years can be referred to by so quiet and so dignified a term as "problem." Complex and appalling it surely was. Goths and Huns, Vandals and Danes, Angles, Saxons, Jutes—could any prophet foresee that a vestige of law and order, of civilization and refinement would remain after this clumsy horde of wild barbarians had swept over Europe?

"Where is somebody'll give me some white for all this yellow?" cries one with his hands full of the gold from one of those magnificent monuments of antiquity which he and his tribe had just pillaged and demolished. Says the historian: "Their history is like a history of kites and crows." Tacitus writes: "To shout, to drink, to caper about, to feel their veins heated and swollen with wine, to hear and see around them the riot of the orgy, this was the first need of the barbarians. The heavy human brute gluts himself with sensations and with noise."

Taine describes them as follows:

"Huge white bodies, cool-blooded, with fierce blue eyes, reddish flaxen hair; ravenous stomachs, filled with meat and cheese, heated by strong drinks. Brutal drunken pirates and robbers, they dashed to sea in their two-sailed barks, landed anywhere, killed everything; and, having sacrificed in honor of their gods the tithe of all their prisoners, leaving behind the red light of their burning, went farther on to begin again."

A certain litany of the time reads: "From the fury of the Jutes, Good Lord deliver us." "Elgiva, the wife of one of their kings," says a chronicler of the time, "they hamstrung and subjected to the death she deserved;" and their heroes are frequently represented as tearing out the heart of their human victim and eating it while it still quivered with life.

A historian of the time, quoted by Taine, says it was the custom to buy men and women in all parts of England and to carry them to Ireland for sale. The buyers usually made the women pregnant and took them to market in that condition to ensure a better price. "You might have seen," continues the historian, "long files of young people of both sexes and of great beauty, bound with ropes and daily exposed for sale. They sold as slaves in this manner, their nearest relatives and even their own children."

What could civilization hope to do with such a swarm of sensuous, bloodthirsty vipers? Assimilation was horrible to contemplate. They will drag us to their level, quoth the culture of the times. Deportation was out of the question; and there was no need to talk of their emigrating. The fact is, the barbarians were in no hurry about moving. They didn't even care to colonize. They had come to stay. And Europe had to grapple with her race problem till time and God should solve it.

And how was it solved, and what kind of civilization resulted?

Once more let us go to Guizot. "Take ever so rapid a glance," says he, "at modern Europe and it strikes you at once as diversified, confused, and stormy. All the principles of social organization are found existing together within it; powers temporal, and powers spiritual, the theocratic, monarchic, aristocratic, and democratic elements, all classes of society *in a state of continual struggle* without any one having sufficient force to master the others and take sole possession of society." Then as to the result of this conflict of forces: "Incomparably more rich and diversified than the ancient, European civilization has within it the promise of *perpetual progress*. It has now endured more than fifteen centuries and in all that time has been in a state of progression, not so rapidly as the Greek nor yet so ephemeral. While in other civilizations the exclusive domination of a principle (*or race*) led to tyranny, in Europe the diversity of social elements (*growing out of the contact of different races*), the incapability of any one to exclude the rest, gave birth to the liberty which now prevails. This inability of the various principles to exterminate one another compelled each to endure the others and made it necessary for them in order to live in common to enter into a sort of mutual understanding. Each consented to have only that part of civilization which equitably fell to its share. Thus, while everywhere else the predominance of one principle produced tyranny, the variety and warfare of the elements of European civilization gave birth to *reciprocity and liberty*."

There is no need to quote further. This is enough to show that the law holds good in sociology as in the world of matter, *that equilibrium, not repression among conflicting forces is the condition of natural harmony, of permanent progress, and of universal freedom*. That exclusiveness and selfishness in a family, in a community, or in a nation is suicidal to progress. Caste and prejudice mean immobility. One race predominance means death. The community that closes its gates against foreign talent can never hope to advance beyond a certain point. Resolve to keep out foreigners and you keep out progress. Home talent develops its one idea and then dies. Like the century plant it produces its one flower, brilliant and beautiful it may be, but it lasts only for a night. Its forces have exhausted themselves in that one effort. Nothing remains but to wither and to rot.

It was the Chinese wall that made China in 1800 A. D. the same as China in the days of Confucius. Its women have not even yet learned that they need not bandage their feet if they do not relish it. The world has rolled on, but within that wall the thoughts, the fashions, the art, the tradition, and the beliefs are those of a thousand years ago. Until very recently, the Chinese were wholly out of the current of human progress. They were like gray headed infants—a man of eighty years with the concepts and imaginings of a babe of eight months. A civilization measured by thousands of years with a development that might be comprised within as many days—arrested development due to exclusive living.

But European civilization, rich as it was compared to Asiatic types, was still not the consummation of the ideal of human possibilities. One more degree westward the hand on the dial points. In Europe there was conflict, but the elements crystallized out in isolated nodules, so to speak. Italy has her dominant principle, Spain hers, France hers, England hers, and so on. The proximity is close enough for interaction and mutual restraint, though the acting forces are at different points. To preserve the balance of power, which is nothing more than the equilibrium of warring elements, England can be trusted to keep an eye on her beloved step-relation-in-law, Russia,—and Germany no doubt can be relied on to look after France and some others. It is not, however, till the scene changes and America is made the theater of action, that the interplay of forces narrowed down to a single platform.

Hither came Cavalier and Roundhead, Baptist and Papist, Quaker, Ritualist, Freethinker and Mormon, the conservative Tory, the liberal Whig, and the radical Independent,—the Spaniard, the Frenchman, the Englishman, the Italian, the Chinaman, the African, Swedes, Russians, Huns, Bohemians, Gypsies, Irish, Jews. Here surely was a seething caldron of conflicting elements. Religious intolerance and political hatred, race prejudice and caste pride—

> "Double, double, toil and trouble;
> Fire burn and cauldron bubble."

Conflict, Conflict, Conflict.

America for Americans! This is the white man's country! The Chinese must go, shrieks the exclusionist. Exclude the Italians! Colonize the blacks in Mexico or deport them to Africa. Lynch, suppress, drive out, kill out! America for Americans!

"*Who are Americans?*" comes rolling back from ten million throats. Who are to do the packing and delivering of the goods? Who are the homefolks and who are the strangers? Who are the absolute and original tenants in fee-simple?

The red men used to be owners of the soil,—but they are about to be pushed over into the Pacific Ocean. They, perhaps, have the best right to call themselves "Americans" by law of primogeniture. They are at least the oldest inhabitants of whom we can at present identify any traces. If early settlers from abroad merely are meant and it is only a question of squatters' rights—why, the Mayflower, a pretty venerable institution, landed in the year of Grace 1620, and the first delegation from Africa just one year ahead of that,—in 1619. The first settlers seem to have been almost as much mixed as we are on this point; and it does not seem at all easy to decide just what individuals we mean when we yell "America for the Americans." At least the cleavage cannot be made by hues and noses, if we are to seek for the genuine F. F. V.'s as the inhabitants best entitled to the honor of that name.

The fact is this nation was foreordained to conflict from its incipiency. Its elements were predestined from their birth to an irrepressible clash followed by the stable equilibrium of opposition. Exclusive possession belongs to none. There never was a point in its history when it did. There was never a time since America became a nation when there were not more than one race, more than one party, more than one belief contending for supremacy. Hence no one is or can be supreme. All interests must be consulted, all claims conciliated. Where a hundred free forces are lustily clamoring for recognition and each wrestling mightily for the mastery, individual tyrannies must inevitably be chiselled down, individual bigotries worn smooth and malleable, individual prejudices either obliterated or concealed. America is not from choice more than of necessity republic in form and democratic in administration. The will of the majority must rule simply because no class, no family, no individual has ever been able to prove sufficient political legitimacy to impose their yoke on the country. All attempts at establishing oligarchy must be made by wheedling and cajoling, pretending that not supremacy but service is sought. The nearest approach to outspoken self-assertion is in the conciliatory tones of candid compromise. "I will let you enjoy that if you will not hinder me in the pursuit of this" has been the American sovereign's home policy since his first Declaration of Independence was inscribed as his policy abroad. Compromise and concession, liberality and toleration were the conditions of the nation's birth and are the *sine qua non* of its continued existence. A general amnesty and universal reciprocity are the only *modus vivendi* in a nation whose every citizen is his own king, his own priest and his own pope.

De Tocqueville, years ago, predicted that republicanism must fail in America. But if republicanism fails, America fails, and somehow I can not think this colossal stage was erected for a tragedy. I must confess to being an optimist on the subject of my country. It is true we are too busy making history, and have been for some years past, to be able to write history yet, or to understand and interpret it. Our range of vision is too short for us to focus and image our conflicts. Indeed Von Holtz, the clearest headed of calm spectators, says he doubts if the history of American conflict can be written yet even by a disinterested foreigner. The clashing of arms and the din of battle, the smoke of cannon and the heat of combat, are not yet cleared away sufficiently for us to have the judicial vision of historians. Our jottings are like newspaper reports written in the saddle, mid prancing steeds and roaring artillery.

But of one thing we may he sure: the God of battles is in the conflicts of history. The evolution of civilization is His care, eternal progress His delight. As the European was higher and grander than the Asiatic, so will American civilization be broader and deeper and closer to the purposes of the Eternal than any the world has yet seen. This the last page is to mark the climax of history, the bright consummate flower unfolding *charity toward all and malice toward none,*—the final triumph of universal reciprocity born of universal conflict with forces that cannot be exterminated. Here at last is an arena in which every agony has a voice and free speech. Not a spot where no wrong can exist, but where each feeblest interest can cry with Themistocles, "*Strike, but hear me!*" Here you will not see as in Germany women hitched to a cart with donkeys; not perhaps because men are more chivalrous here than there, but because woman can speak. Here labor will not be starved and ground to powder, because the laboring man can make himself heard. Here races that are weakest can, *if they so elect*, make themselves felt.

The supremacy of one race,—the despotism of a class or the tyranny of an individual can not ultimately prevail on a continent held in equilibrium by such conflicting forces and by so many and such strong fibred races as there are struggling on this soil. Never in America shall one man dare to say as Germany's somewhat bumptious emperor is fond of proclaiming: "There is only one master in the country and I am he. I shall suffer no other beside me. Only to God and my conscience am I accountable." The strength of the opposition tones down and polishes off all such ugly excrescencies as that. "I am the State," will never be proclaimed above a whisper on a platform where there is within arm's length another just as strong, possibly stronger, who holds, or would like to hold that identical proposition with reference to himself. In this arena then is to be the last death struggle of political tyranny, of religious bigotry, and intellectual intolerance, of caste illiberality and class exclusiveness. And the last monster that shall be throttled forever methinks is race prejudice. Men will here learn that a race, as a family, may be true to itself without seeking to exterminate all others. That for the note of the feeblest there is room, nay a positive need, in the harmonies of God. That the principles of true democracy are founded in universal reciprocity, and that "A man's a man" was written when God first stamped His own image and superscription on His child and breathed into his nostrils the breath of life. And I confess I can pray for no nobler destiny for my country than that it may be the stage, however far distant in the future, whereon these ideas and principles shall ultimately mature; and culminating here at whatever cost of production shall go forth hence to dominate the world.

Methought I saw a mighty conflagration, plunging and heaving, surging and seething, smoking and rolling over this American continent. Strong men and wise men stand helpless in mute consternation. Empty headed babblers add the din of their bray to the crashing and crackling of the flames. But the hungry flood rolls on. The air is black with smoke and cinders. The sky is red with lurid light. Forked tongues of fiery flame dart up and lick the pale stars, and seem to laugh at men's feebleness and frenzy. As I look on I think of Schiller's sublime characterization of fire: "Frightful becomes this God-power, when it snatches itself free from fetters and stalks majestically forth on its own career—the free daughter of Nature." Ingenuity is busy with newly patented snuffers all warranted to extinguish the flame. The street gamin with a hooked wire pulls out a few nuggets that chanced to be lying on the outskirts where they were cooked by the heat; and gleefully cries "What a nice fire to roast my chestnuts," and like little Jack Horner, "what a nice boy am I!"

Meantime this expedient, that expedient, the other expedient is suggested by thinkers and theorizers hoping to stifle the angry, roaring, devouring demon and allay the mad destruction.

> "Wehe wenn sie losgelassen,
>   Wachsend ohne Widerstand,

> Durch die volkbelebten Gassen
> Walzt den ungeheuren Brand!"

But the strength of the Omnipotent is in it. The hand of God is leading it on. It matters not whether you and I in mad desperation cast our quivering bodies into it as our funeral pyre; or whether, like the street urchins, we pull wires to secure the advantage of the passing moment. We can neither help it nor hinder; only

> "Let thy gold be cast in the furnace,
> Thy red gold, precious and bright.
> Do not fear the hungry fire
> With its caverns of burning light."

If it takes the dearest idol, the pet theory or the darling 'ism,' the pride, the selfishness, the prejudices, the exclusiveness, the bigotry and intolerance, the conceit of self, of race, or of family superiority,—nay, if it singe from thee thy personal gratifications in thy distinction by birth, by blood, by sex—everything,—and leave thee nothing but thy naked manhood, solitary and unadorned,—let them go—let them go!

> "And thy gold shall return more precious,
> Free from every spot and stain,
> For gold must be tried by fire."

And the heart of nations must be tried by pain; and their polish, their true culture must be wrought in through conflict.

Has America a Race Problem?

Yes.

What are you going to do about it?

Let it alone and mind my own business. It is God's problem and He will solve it in time. It is deeper than Gehenna. What can you or I do!

Are there then no duties and special lines of thought growing out of the present conditions of this problem?

Certainly there are. *Imprimis;* let every element of the conflict see that it represent a positive force so as to preserve a proper equipoise in the conflict. No shirking, no skulking, no masquerading in another's uniform. Stand by your guns. And be ready for the

charge. The day is coming, and now is, when America must ask
each citizen not "who was your grandfather and what the color of
his cuticle," but *"What can you do?"* Be ready each individual element,—each race, each class, each family, each man to reply *"I
engage to undertake an honest man's share."*

God and time will work the problem. You and I are only to
stand for the quantities *at their best*, which he means us to represent.

Above all, for the love of humanity stop the mouth of those
learned theorizers, the expedient mongers, who come out annually
with their new and improved method of getting the answer and
clearing the slate: amalgamation, deportation, colonization and all
the other ations that were ever devised or dreamt of. If Alexander
wants to be a god, let him; but don't have Alexander hawking his
patent plan for universal deification. If all could or would follow
Alexander's plan, just the niche in the divine cosmos meant for man
would be vacant. And we think that men have a part to play in this
great drama no less than gods, and so if a few are determined to be
white—amen, so be it; but don't let them argue as if there were no
part to be played in life by black men and black women, and as if
to become white were the sole specific and panacea for all the ills
that flesh is heir to—the universal solvent for all America's irrita-
tions. And again, if an American family of whatever condition or
hue takes a notion to reside in Africa or in Mexico, or in the isles
of the sea, it is most un-American for any power on this continent
to seek to gainsay or obstruct their departure; but on the other
hand, no power or element of power on this continent, least of all
a self-constituted tribunal of "recent arrivals," possesses the right to
begin figuring beforehand to calculate what it would require *to send*
ten millions of citizens, whose ancestors have wrought here from
the planting of the nation, to the same places at so much per head—
at least till some one has consulted those heads.

We would not deprecate the fact, then, that America has a Race
Problem. It is guaranty of the perpetuity and progress of her institutions, and insures the breadth of her culture and the symmetry of
her development. More than all, let us not disparage the factor
which the Negro is appointed to contribute to that problem.
America needs the Negro for ballast if for nothing else. His tropical
warmth and spontaneous emotionalism may form no unseemly
counterpart to the cold and calculating Anglo-Saxon. And then his
instinct for law and order, his inborn respect for authority, his

inaptitude for rioting and anarchy, his gentleness and cheerfulness as a laborer, and his deep-rooted faith in God will prove indispensable and invaluable elements in a nation menaced as America is by anarchy, socialism, communism, and skepticism poured in with all the jail birds from the continents of Europe and Asia. I believe with our own Dr. Crummell that "the Almighty does not preserve, rescue, and build up a lowly people merely for ignoble ends." And the historian of American civilization will yet congratulate this country that she has had a Race Problem and that descendants of the black race furnished one of its largest factors.

THE NEGRO AS PRESENTED IN
AMERICAN LITERATURE

FOR NATIONS AS for individuals, a product, to be worthy the term literature, must contain something characteristic and *sui generis*.

So long as America remained a mere English colony, drawing all her life and inspiration from the mother country, it may well be questioned whether there was such a thing as American literature. "Who ever reads an American book?" it was scornfully asked in the eighteenth century. Imitation is the worst of suicides; it cuts the nerve of originality and condemns to mediocrity: and 'twas not till the pen of our writers was dipped in the life blood of their own nation and pictured out its own peculiar heart throbs and agonies that the world cared to listen. The nightingale and the skylark had to give place to the mocking bird, the bobolink and the whippoor-will, the heather and the blue bells of Britain, to our own golden-rod and daisy; the insular and monarchic customs and habits of thought of old England must develop into the broader, looser, freer swing of democratic America, before her contributions to the world of thought could claim the distinction of individuality and gain an appreciative hearing.

And so our writers have succeeded in becoming national and representative in proportion as they have from year to year entered more and more fully, and more and more sympathetically, into the distinctive life of their nation, and endeavored to reflect and picture its homeliest pulsations and its elemental components. And so in all the arts, as men have gradually come to realize that

> Nothing useless is or low
> Each thing in its place is best,

and have wrought into their products, lovingly and impartially and reverently, every type, every tint, every tone that they felt or saw or heard, just to that degree have their expressions, whether by pen or brush or rhythmic cadence, adequately and simply given voice to the thought of Nature around them. No man can prophesy with another's parable. For each of us truth means merely the re-presentation of the sensations and experiences of our personal environment, colored and vivified—fused into consistency and crytallized into individuality in the crucible of our own feelings and imaginations. The mind of genius is merely the brook, picturing back its own tree and bush and bit of sky and cloud ensparkled by individual salts and sands and rippling motion. And paradoxical as it may seem, instead of making us narrow and provincial, this trueness to one's habitat, this appreciative eye and ear for the tints and voices of one's own little wood serves but to usher us into the eternal galleries and choruses of God. It is only through the unclouded perception of our tiny "part" that we can come to harmonize with the "stupendous whole," and in order to do this our sympathies must be finely attuned and quick to vibrate under the touch of the commonplace and vulgar no less than at the hand of the elegent and refined. Nothing natural can be wholly unworthy; and we do so at our peril, if, what God has cleansed we presume to call common or unclean. Nature's language is not writ in cipher. Her notes are always simple and sensuous, and the very meanest recesses and commonest byways are fairly deafening with her sermons and songs. It is only when we ourselves are out of tune through our pretentiousness and self-sufficiency, or are blinded and rendered insensate by reason of our foreign and unnatural "cultivation" that we miss her meanings and inadequately construe her multiform lessons.

For two hundred and fifty years there was in the American commonwealth a great *silent* factor. Though in themselves simple and unique their offices were those of the barest utility. Imported merely to be hewers of wood and drawers of water, no artist for many a generation thought them worthy the sympathetic study of a model. No Shakespeare arose to distil from their unmatched personality and unparalleled situations the exalted poesy and crude grandeur of an immortal Caliban. Distinct in color, original in temperament, simple and unconventionalized in thought and action their spiritual development and impressionability under their novel environment would have furnished, it might seem, as interesting a study in psychology for the poetic pen, as would the gorges of the Yosemite to the inspired pencil. Full of vitality and natural elasticity, the severest persecution and oppression could not kill them out or even sour their temper. With massive brawn and indefatigable endurance they wrought under burning suns and chilling blasts, in swamps and marshes,—they cleared the forests, tunneled mountains, threaded the land with railroads, planted, picked and ginned the cotton, produced the rice and the sugar for the markets of the world. Without money and without price they poured their hearts' best blood into the enriching and developing of this country. *They wrought but were silent.*

The most talked about of all the forces in this diversified civilization, they seemed the great American fact, the one objective reality, on which scholars sharpened their wits, at which orators and statesmen fired their eloquence, and from which, after so long a time, authors, with varied success and truthfulness have begun at last to draw subjects and models. Full of imagination and emotion, their sensuous pictures of the "New Jerusalem," "the golden slippers," "the long white robe," "the pearly gates," etc., etc., seem fairly to steam with tropical luxuriance and naive abandon. The paroxysms of religious fervor into which this simple-minded, child-like race were thrown by the contemplation of Heaven and rest and freedom, would have melted into sympathy and tender pity if not into love, a race less cold and unresponsive than the one with which they were thrown in closest contact. There was something truly poetic in their weird moanings, their fitful gleams of hope and trust, flickering amidst the darkness of their wailing helplessness, their strange sad songs, the half coherent ebullitions of souls in pain, which become, the more they are studied, at once the wonder and the despair of musical critics and imitators. And if one had the insight and the simplicity to gather together, to digest and assimilate these original lispings of an unsophisticated people while they were yet close—so close—to nature and to nature's God, there is material here, one might almost believe, as rich, as unhackneyed, as original and distinctive as ever inspired a Homer, or a Cædmon or other simple genius of a people's infancy and lisping childhood.

In the days of their bitterest persecution, their patient endurance and Christian manliness inspired Uncle Tom's Cabin, which revolutionized the thought of the world on the subject of slavery and at once placed its author in the front rank of the writers of her country and age. Here at last was a work which England could not parallel. Here was a work indigenous to American soil and characteristic of the country—a work which American forces alone could have produced. The subject was at once seen to be fresh and interesting to the world as well as national and peculiar to America; and so it has since been eagerly cultivated by later writers with widely varying degrees of fitness and success.

By a rough classification, authors may be separated into two groups: first, those in whom the artistic or poetic instinct is uppermost—those who write to please—or rather who write because *they* please; who simply paint what they see, as naturally, as instinctively, and as irresistibly as the bird sings—with no thought of an audience—singing because it loves to sing,—singing because God, nature, truth sings through it. For such writers, to be true to themselves and true to Nature is the only canon. They cannot warp a character or distort a fact in order to prove a point. They have nothing to prove. All who care to, may listen while they make the woods resound with their glad sweet carolling; and the listeners may draw their own conclusions as to the meaning of the cadences of this minor strain, or that hushed and almost awful note of rage or despair. And the myriad-minded multitude attribute their myriad-fold impressions to the myriad-minded soul by which they have severally been enchanted, each in his own way according to what he brings to the witching auditorium. But the singer sings on with his hat before his face, unmindful, it may be unconscious, of the varied strains reproduced from him in the multitudinous echoes of the crowd. Such was Shakespeare, such was George Eliot, such was Robert Browning. Such, in America, was Poe, was Bryant, was Longfellow; and such, in his own degree perhaps, is Mr. Howells.

In the second group belong the preachers,—whether of righteousness or unrighteousness,—all who have an idea to propagate, no matter in what form their talent enables them to clothe it, whether poem, novel, or sermon,—all those writers with a purpose or a lesson, who catch you by the buttonhole and pommel you over the shoulder till you are forced to give assent in order to escape their vociferations; or they may lure you into listening with the soft music of the siren's tongue—no matter what the expedient to catch and hold your attention, they mean to fetter you with their one idea, whatever it is, and make you, if possible, ride their hobby. In this group I would place Milton in much of his writing, Carlyle in all of his, often our own Whittier, the great reformer-poet, and Lowell;

together with such novelists as E. P. Roe, Bellamy, Tourgee and some others.

Now in my judgment writings of the first class will be the ones to withstand the ravages of time. 'Isms' have their day and pass away. New necessities arise with new conditions and the emphasis has to be shifted to suit the times. No finite mind can grasp and give out the whole circle of truth. We do well if we can illuminate just the tiny arc which we occupy and should be glad that the next generation will not need the lessons we try so assiduously to hammer into this. In the evolution of society, as the great soul of humanity builds it "more lofty chambers," the old shell and slough of didactic teaching must be left behind and forgotten. The world for instance has outgrown, I suspect, those passages of Paradise Lost in which Milton makes the Almighty Father propound the theology of a seventeenth century Presbyterian. But a passage like the one in which Eve with guileless innocence describes her first sensations on awaking into the world is as perennial as man.

> "That day I oft remember, when from sleep
>   I first awaked and found myself reposed
>   Under a shade on flowers, much wondering where
>   And what I was, whence thither brought and how.
>   Not distant far from thence a murmuring sound
>   Of waters issued from a cave, and spread
>   Into a liquid plain, then stood unmoved
>   Pure as the expanse of Heaven;
>   I thither went
>   With unexperienced thought and laid me down
>   On the green bank, to look into the clear
>   Smooth lake that to me seemed another sky.
>   As I bent down to look, just opposite
>   A shape within the watery gleam appeared,
>   Bending to look on me; I started back,
>   It started back; but pleased I soon returned,
>   Pleased it returned as soon with answering looks
>   Of sympathy and love; there I had fixed
>   Mine eyes till now,—and pined with vain desire,
>   Had not a voice thus warned me.
>   'What thou seest,
>   What there thou seest, fair creature, is thyself;

With thee it came and goes; but follow me,
And I will bring thee where no shadow stays
Thy coming and thy soft embraces.'
                    What could I do but follow straight
Invisibly thus led?
Till I espied thee, fair indeed and tall,
Under a plantain; yet methought less fair,
Less winning soft, less amiably mild
Than that smooth watery image; back I turned
Thou following criedst aloud, 'Return, fair Eve,
Whom fliest thou? whom thou fliest, of him thou art.
Part of my soul, I seek thee, and thee claim
My other half.'"

This will never cease to throb and thrill as long as man is man and woman is woman.

Now owing to the problematical position at present occupied by descendants of Africans in the American social polity,—growing, I presume, out of the continued indecision in the mind of the more powerful descendants of the Saxons as to whether it is expedient to apply the maxims of their religion to their civil and political relationships,—most of the writers who have hitherto attempted a portrayal of life and customs among the darker race have belonged to our class II: they have all, more or less, had a point to prove or a mission to accomplish, and thus their art has been almost uniformly perverted to serve their ends; and, to add to their disadvantage, most, if not all the writers on this line have been but partially acquainted with the life they wished to delineate and through sheer ignorance ofttimes, as well as from design occasionally, have not been able to put themselves in the darker man's place. The art of "thinking one's self imaginatively into the experiences of others" is not given to all, and it is impossible to acquire it without a background and a substratum of sympathetic knowledge. Without this power our portraits are but death's heads or caricatures and no amount of cudgeling can put into them the movement and reality of life. Not many have had Mrs. Stowe's power because not many have studied with Mrs. Stowe's humility and love. They forget that underneath the black man's form and behavior there is the great bed-rock of humanity, the key to which is the same that unlocks every tribe and kindred of the nations of earth. Some have taken

up the subject with a view to establishing evidences of ready for-
mulated theories and preconceptions; and, blinded by their prejudices and antipathies, have altogether abjured all candid and careful
study. Others with flippant indifference have performed a few
psychological experiments on their cooks and coachmen, and with
astounding egotism, and powers of generalization positively bewil-
dering, forthwith aspire to enlighten the world with dissertations on
racial traits of the Negro. A few with really kind intentions and a
sincere desire for information have approached the subject as a
clumsy microscopist, not quite at home with his instrument, might
study a new order of beetle or bug. Not having focused closely
enough to obtain a clear-cut view, they begin by telling you that
all colored people look exactly alike and end by noting down every
chance contortion or idiosyncrasy as a race characteristic. Some of
their conclusions remind one of the enterprising German on a tour
of research and self improvement through Great Britain, who rec-
ommended his favorite sauer kraut both to an Irishman, whom he
found sick with fever, and to a Scotchman, who had a cold. On
going that way subsequently and finding the Scotchman well and
the Irishman dead, he writes: *Mem.—Sauer kraut good for the Scotch
but death to the Irish.*

This criticism is not altered by our grateful remembrance of
those who have heroically taken their pens to champion the black
man's cause. But even here we may remark that a painter may be
irreproachable in motive and as benevolent as an angel in intention,
nevertheless we have a right to compare his copy with the original
and point out in what respects it falls short or is overdrawn; and he
should thank us for doing so.

It is in no captious spirit, therefore, that we note a few contributions to this phase of American literature which have been made
during the present decade; we shall try to estimate their weight,
their tendency, their truthfulness and their lessons, if any, for
ourselves.

Foremost among the champions of the black man's cause
through the medium of fiction must be mentioned Albion W.
Tourgee. No man deserves more the esteem and appreciation of
the colored people of this country for his brave words. For ten years
he has stood almost alone as the enthusiastic advocate, not of charity and dole to the Negro, but of justice. The volumes he has written upon the subject have probably been read by from five to ten

millions of the American people. Look over his list consecrated to one phase or another of the subject: "A Fool's Errand," "A Royal Gentleman," "Bricks without Straw," "An Appeal to Cæsar," "Hot Ploughshares," "Pactolus Prime,"—over three thousand pages—enough almost for a life work, besides an almost interminable quantity published in periodicals.

Mr. Tourgee essays to paint life with the coloring of fiction, and yet, we must say, we do not think him a novelist primarily; that is, novel making with him seems to be a mere incident, a convenient vehicle through which to convey those burning thoughts which he is constantly trying to impress upon the people of America, whether in lecture, stump speech, newspaper column or magazine article. His power is not that already referred to of thinking himself imaginatively into the experiences of others. He does not create many men of many minds. All his offspring are little Tourgees—they preach his sermons and pray his prayers.

In "Pactolus Prime," for example, one of his latest, his hero, a colored bootblack in a large hotel, is none other than the powerful, impassioned, convinced and convincing lecturer, Judge Tourgee himself, done over in ebony. His caustic wit, his sledge hammer logic, his incisive criticism, his righteous indignation, all reflect the irresistible arguments of the great pleader for the Negro; and all the incidents are arranged to enable this bootblack to impress on senators and judges, lawyers, and divines, his plea for justice to the Negro, along with the blacking and shine which he skillfully puts on their aristocratic toes. And so with all the types which Mr. Tourgee presents—worthy or pitiful ones always—they uniformly preach or teach, convict or convert. Artistic criticism aside, it is mainly as a contribution to polemic literature in favor of the colored man that most of Tourgee's works will be judged; and we know of no one who can more nearly put himself in the Negro's place in resenting his wrongs and pleading for his rights. In presenting truth from the colored American's standpoint Mr. Tourgee excels, we think, in fervency and frequency of utterance any living writer, white or colored. Mr. Cable is brave and just. He wishes to see justice done in the Freedman's case in equity, and we honor and revere him for his earnest manly efforts towards that end. But Mr. Cable does not forget (I see no reason why he should, of course,) that he is a white man, a Southerner and an ex-soldier in the Confederate army. To use his own words, he writes, "with an admiration and affection for the South, that for justice and sincerity yield to none; in a spirit of faithful sonship to a Southern state." Of course this but proves his sincerity, illustrates his candor, and adds weight to the axiomatic justice of a cause which demands such support from a thoroughly disinterested party, or rather a party whose interest and sympathy and affection must be all on the side he criticises and condemns. The passion of the partisan and the bias of the aggrieved can never be charged against him. Mr. Cable's is the impartiality of the judge who condemns his own son or cuts off his own arm. His attitude is judicial, convincing, irreproachable throughout.

Not only the Christian conscience of the South, but also its enlightened self-interest is unquestionably on the side of justice and manly dealing toward the black man; and one can not help feeling that a cause which thus enlists the support and advocacy of the "better self" of a nation must ultimately be invincible: and Mr. Cable, in my judgment, embodies and represents that Christian conscience and enlightened self-interest of the hitherto silent South; he vocalizes and inspires its better self. To him the dishonesty and inhumanity there practiced against the black race is a blot on the scutcheon of that fair land and doomed to bring in its wake untold confusion, disaster, and disgrace. From his calm elevation he sees the impending evil, and with loving solicitude urges his countrymen to flee the wrath to come. Mr. Tourgee, on the other hand, speaks with all the eloquence and passion of the aggrieved party himself. With his whip of fine cords he pitilessly scourges the inconsistencies, the weaknesses and pettiness of the black man's persecutors. The fire is burning within him, he cannot but speak. He has said himself that he deserves no credit for speaking and writing on this subject, for it has taken hold of him and possesses him to the exclusion of almost everything else. Necessity is laid upon him. Not more bound was Saul of Tarsus to consecrate his fiery eloquence to the cause of the persecuted Nazarene than is this white man to throw all the weight of his powerful soul into the plea for justice and Christianity in this American anomaly and huge inconsistency. Not many colored men would have attempted Tourgee's brave defense of Reconstruction and the alleged corruption of Negro supremacy, more properly termed the period of white sullenness and desertion of duty. Not many would have dared, fearlessly as he did, to arraign this country for an enormous pecuniary debt to the colored man for the two hundred and forty-seven years of unpaid labor of his ancestors. Not many could so determinedly have held up the glass of the real Christianity before these believers in a white Christ and these preachers of the gospel, "Suffer the little *white* children to come unto me." We all see the glaring inconsistency and feel the burning shame. We appreciate the incongruity and the indignity of having to stand forever hat in hand as beggars, or be shoved aside as intruders in a country whose resources have been opened up by the unrequited toil of our forefathers. We know that our bill is a true one—that the debt is as real as to any pensioners of our government. But the principles of patience and forbearance, of meekness and charity, have become so ingrained in the Negro character that there is hardly enough self-assertion left to ask as our right that a part of the country's surplus wealth be *loaned* for the education of our children; even though we know that our present poverty is due to the fact that the toil of the last quarter century enriched these coffers, but left us the heirs of crippled, deformed, frost-bitten, horny-handed and empty handed mothers and fathers. Oh, the shame of it!

A coward during the war gets a few scratches and bruises—often in *fleeing from the enemy*—and his heirs are handsomely pensioned by his *grateful* country! But these poor wretches stood every man to his post for two hundred and fifty years, digging trenches, building roads, tunneling mountains, clearing away forests, cultivating the soil in the cotton fields and rice swamps till fingers dropped off, toes were frozen, knees twisted, arms stiff and useless—and when their sons and heirs, with the burdens of helpless parents to support, wish to secure enough education to enable them to make a start in life, *their* grateful country sagely deliberates as to the feasibility of sending them to another undeveloped jungle to show off their talent for unlimited pioneer work in strange climes! The Indian, during the entire occupancy of this country by white men, has stood proudly aloof from all their efforts at development, and presented an unbroken front of hostility to the introduction and spread of civilization. The Negro, though brought into the country by force and compelled under the lash to lend his brawn and sturdy sinews to promote its material growth and prosperity, nevertheless with perfect amiability of temper and adaptability of mental structure has quietly and unhesitatingly accepted its standards and fallen in line with its creeds. He adjusts himself just as readily and as appreciatively, it would seem, to the higher and stricter requirements of freedom and citizenship; and although from beginning to end, nettled and goaded under unprecedented provocation, he has never once shown any general disposition to arise in his might and deluge this country with blood or desolate it with burning, as he might have done. It is no argument to charge weakness as the cause of his peaceful submission and to sneer at the "inferiority" of a race who would allow themselves to be made slaves—unrevenged. It *may* be nobler to perish redhanded, to kill as many as your battle axe holds out to hack and then fall with an exultant yell and savage grin of fiendish delight on the hugh pile of bloody corpses,—expiring with the solace and unction of having ten thousand wounds all in front. I don't know. I sometimes think it depends on where you plant your standard and who wears the white plume which your eye inadvertently seeks. If Napoleon is the ideal of mankind, I suppose 'tis only noble to be strong; and true greatness may consist in an adamantine determination never to serve. The greatest race with which I am even partially acquainted, proudly boasts that it has never met another race save as either enemy or victim. They seem to set great store by this fact and I judge it must be immensely noble according to their ideals. But somehow it seems to me that those nations and races who choose the Nazarene for their plumed knight would find some little jarring and variance between such notions and His ideals. There could not be at all times perfect unanimity between Leader and host. A good many of his sayings, it seems to me, would have to be explained away; not a few of his injunctions quietly ignored, and I am not sure but the great bulk of his principles and precepts must after all lie like leaden lumps, an undigested and unassimilable mass on an uneasy overburdened stomach. I find it rather hard to understand these things, and somehow I feel at times as if I have taken hold of the wrong ideal. But then, I suppose, it must be because I have not enough of the spirit that comes with the blood of those grand old *sea kings* (I believe you call them) who shot out in their trusty barks speeding over unknown seas and, like a death-dealing genius, with the piercing eye and bloodthirsty heart of hawk or vulture killed and harried, burned and caroused. This is doubtless all very glorious and noble, and the seed of it must be an excellent thing to have in one's blood. But I haven't it. I frankly admit my limitations. I am hardly capable of appreciating to the full such grand intrepidity,—due of course to the fact that the stock from which I am sprung did not attain that royal kink in its blood ages ago. My tribe has to own kinship with a very tame and unsanguinary individual who, a long time

ago when blue blood was a distilling in the stirring fiery world outside, had no more heroic and daring a thing to do than help a pale
sorrow-marked man as he was toiling up a certain hill at Jerusalem
bearing his own cross whereon he was soon to be ignominiously
nailed. This Cyrenian fellow was used to bearing burdens and he
didn't mind giving a lift over a hard place now and then, with no
idea of doing anything grand or memorable, or that even so much
as his name would be known thereby. And then, too, by a rather
strange coincidence this unwarlike and insignificant kinsman of ours
had his home in a country (the fatherland of all the family) which
had afforded kindly shelter to that same mysterious Stranger, when,
a babe and persecuted by bloody power and heartless jealousy, He
had to flee the land of his birth. And somehow this same country
has in its day done so much fostering and sheltering of that kind—
has watched and hovered over the cradles of religions and given
refuge and comfort to the persecuted, the world weary, the storm
tossed benefactors of mankind so often that she has come to represent nothing stronger or more imposing than the "eternal womanly"
among the nations, and to accept as her mission and ideal, *loving
service* to mankind.

With such antecedents then the black race in America should not
be upbraided for having no taste for blood and carnage. It is the
fault of their constitution that they prefer the judicial awards of
peace and have an eternal patience to abide the bloodless triumph
of right. It is no argument, therefore, when I point to the record of
their physical supremacy—when the homes and helpless ones of
this country were absolutely at the black man's mercy and not a
town laid waste, not a building burned, and *not a woman insulted*—
it is no argument, I say, for you to retort: "*He was a coward; he didn't
dare!*" The facts simply do not show this to have been the case.

Now the tardy conscience of the nation wakes up one bright
morning and is overwhelmed with blushes and stammering confusion because convicted of dishonorable and unkind treatment of *the
Indian;* and there is a wonderful scurrying around among the keep-
ers of the keys to get out more blankets and send out a few primers
for the "*wards.*" While the black man, a faithful son and indefeasible
heir,—who can truthfully say, "Lo, these many years do I serve
thee, neither transgressed I at any time thy commandment, and yet
thou never gavest me a kid that I might make merry with my
friends,"—is snubbed and chilled and made unwelcome at every

merry-making of the family. And when appropriations for education are talked of, the section for which he has wrought and suffered most, actually defeats the needed and desired assistance for fear they may not be able to prevent his getting a fair and equitable share in the distribution.

Oh, the shame of it!

In Pactolus Prime Mr. Tourgee has succeeded incomparably, we think, in photographing and vocalizing the feelings of the colored American in regard to the Christian profession and the pagan practice of the dominant forces in the American government. And as an impassioned denunciation of the heartless and godless spirit of caste founded on color, as a scathing rebuke to weak-eyed Christians who cannot read the golden rule across the color line, as an unanswerable arraignment of unparalleled ingratitude and limping justice in the policy of this country towards the weaker of its two children, that served it so long and so faithfully, the book is destined to live and to furnish an invaluable contribution to this already plethoric department of American literature.

Mr. Cable and Mr. Tourgee represent possibly the most eminent as well as the most prolific among the writers on this subject belonging to the didactic or polemic class. A host of others there are—lesser lights, or of more intermittent coruscations—who have contributed on either side the debate single treatises, numerous magazine articles or newspaper editorials, advocating some one theory some another on the so-called *race problem*. In this group belongs the author of "An Appeal to Pharoah," advocating the deportation absurdity; also the writings of H. W. Grady; "In Plain Black and White," "The Brother in Black," "The South Investigated," "A Defense of the Negro Race," "The Prosperity of the South Dependent on the Elevation of the Negro," "The Old South and the New," "Black and White," etc., etc., among which are included articles from the pen of colored men themselves, such as Mr. Douglass, Dr. Crummell, Dr. Arnett, Dr. Blyden, Dr. Scarborough, Dr. Price, Mr. Fortune, and others. These are champions of the forces on either side. They stand ever at the forefront dealing desperate blows right and left, now fist and skull, now broad-sword and battle-axe, now with the flash and boom of artillery; while the little fellows run out ever and anon from the ranks and deliver a telling blow between the eyes of an antagonist. All are wrought up to a high tension, some are blinded with passion, others appalled with dread,—all sincerely feel the reality of their own vision and earnestly hope to compel their world to see with their eyes. Such works, full of the fever and heat of debate belong to the turmoil and turbulence of the time. A hundred years from now they may be interesting history, throwing light on a feature of these days which, let us hope, will then be hardly intelligible to an American citizen not over fifty years old.

Among our artists for art's sweet sake, Mr. Howells has recently tried his hand also at painting the Negro, attempting merely a side light in half tones, on his life and manners; and I think the unanimous verdict of the subject is that, in this single department at least, Mr. Howells does not know what he is talking about. And yet I do not think we should quarrel with *An Imperative Duty* because it lacks the earnestness and bias of a special pleader. Mr. Howells merely meant to press the button and give one picture from American life involving racial complications. The kodak does no more; it cannot preach sermons or solve problems.

Besides, the portrayal of Negro characteristics was by no means the main object of the story, which was rather meant, I judge, to be a thumb nail sketch containing a psychological study of a morbidly sensitive conscience hectoring over a weak and vacillating will and fevered into increased despotism by reading into its own life and consciousness the analyses and terrible retributions of fiction,— a product of the Puritan's uncompromising sense of "*right though the heavens fall,*" irritated and kept sore by being unequally yoked with indecision and cowardice. Of such strokes Mr. Howells is undoubtedly master. It is true there is little point and no force of character about the beautiful and irresponsible young heroine; but as that is an attainment of so many of Mr. Howells' models, it is perhaps not to be considered as illustrating any racial characteristics. I cannot help sharing, however, the indignation of those who resent the picture in the colored church,—"evidently," Mr. Howells assures us, "representing *the best colored society*"; where the horrified young prig, Rhoda Aldgate, meets nothing but the frog-like countenances and cat-fish mouths, the musky exhalations and the "bress de Lawd, Honey," of an uncultivated people. It is just here that Mr. Howells fails—and fails because he gives only a half truth, and that a partisan half truth. One feels that he had no business to attempt a subject of which he knew so little, or for which he cared so little. There is one thing I would like to say to my white fellow countrymen, and especially to those who dabble in ink and affect to discuss the

Negro; and yet I hesitate because I feel it is a fact which persons of the finer sensibilities and more delicate perceptions must know instinctively: namely, that it is an insult to humanity and a sin against God to publish any such sweeping generalizations of a race on such meager and superficial information. We meet it at every turn—this obtrusive and offensive vulgarity, this gratuitous sizing up of the Negro and conclusively writing down his equation, sometimes even among his ardent friends and bravest defenders. Were I not afraid of falling myself into the same error that I am condemning, I would say it seems an *Anglo Saxon characteristic* to have such overweening confidence in his own power of induction that there is no equation which he would acknowledge to be indeterminate, however many unknown quantities it may possess.

Here is an extract from Dr. Mayo, a thoroughly earnest man and sincerely friendly, as I believe, to the colored people.

> "Among these women are as many grades of native, intellectual, moral and executive force as among the white people. The plantations of the Gulf, the Atlantic coast and the Mississippi bottoms swarm with negro women who seem hardly lifted above the brutes. I know a group of young colored women, many of them accomplished teachers, who bear themselves as gently and with as varied womanly charms as any score of ladies in the land. The one abyss of perdition *to this class* is the slough of unchastity in which, *as a race* they still flounder, half conscious that it is a slough—the double inheritance of savage Africa and slavery."

Now there may be one side of a truth here, yet who but a self-confident Anglo Saxon would dare make such a broad unblushing statement about a people *as a race?* Some developments brought to light recently through the scientific Christianity and investigating curiosity of Dr. Parkhurst may lead one to suspect the need of missionary teaching to "elevate" the white race; and yet I have too much respect for the autonomy of races, too much reverence for the collective view of God's handiwork to speak of any such condition, however general, as characterizing *the race*. The colored people do not object to the adequate and truthful portrayal of types of their race in whatever degree of the scale of civilization, or of social and moral development, is consonant with actual facts or possibilities. As Mr. Howells himself says, "A man can be anything along the vast range from angel to devil, and without living either the good thing or the bad thing in which his fancy dramatizes him, he can perceive it"—and I would add, can appreciate and even enjoy its delineation by the artist. The average Englishman takes no exception to the humorous caricatures of Dickens or to the satires and cynicisms of Thackeray. The Quilps and the Bernsteins are but strongly developed negatives of our universal human nature on the dark side. We recognize them as genre sketches,—and with the Agneses and Esthers and Aunt Lamberts as foils and correctives, we can appreciate them accordingly: while we do not believe ourselves to be the original of the portrait, there is enough sympathy and fellow feeling for the character to prevent our human relationship from being outraged and insulted. But were Dickens to introduce an average scion of his countrymen to a whole congregation of *Quilps*, at the same time sagely informing him that these represented *the best there was* of English life and morals, I strongly suspect the charming author would be lifted out on the toe of said average Englishman's boot, in case there shouldn't happen to be a good horsewhip handy.

Our grievance then is not that we are not painted as angels of light or as goody-goody Sunday-school developments; but we do claim that a man whose acquaintanceship is so slight that he cannot even discern diversities of individuality, has no right or authority to hawk "the only true and authentic" pictures of a race of human beings. Mr. Howells' point of view is precisely that of a white man who sees colored people at long range or only in certain capacities. His conclusions about the colored man are identical with the impressions that will be received and carried abroad by foreigners from all parts of the globe, who shall attend our Columbian Exposition for instance, and who, through the impartiality and generosity of our white countrymen, will see colored persons only as bootblacks and hotel waiters, grinning from ear to ear and bowing and courtesying for the extra tips. In the same way Mr. Howells has met colored persons in hotels or on the commons promenading and sparking, or else acting as menials and lazzaroni. He has not seen, and therefore cannot be convinced that there exists a quiet, self-respecting, dignified class of easy life and manners (save only where it crosses the roughness of their white fellow countrymen's barbarity) of cultivated tastes and habits, and with no more in common with the class of his acquaintance than the accident of complexion,—beyond a sympathy with their wrongs, or a resentment at being socially and morally classified with them, according as the principle of altruism or of self love is dominant in the individual.

I respectfully submit that there is hardly a colored church in any considerable city in this country, which could be said in any sense to represent *the best colored society*, in which Rhoda Aldgate could not have seen, when she opened her eyes, persons as quietly and as becomingly dressed, as cultivated in tone and as refined in manner, as herself; persons, too, as sensitive to rough contact and as horribly alive as she could be (though they had known it from childhood) to the galling distinctions in this country which insist on *levelling down* all individuals more or less related to the Africans. So far from the cringing deference which Mr. Howells paints as exhibited to "the young white lady," in nine cases out of ten the congregation would have supposed intuitively that she was a quadroon, so far from the unusual was her appearance and complexion. In not a few such colored churches would she have found young women of aspiration and intellectual activity with whom she could affiliate without nausea and from whom she could learn a good many lessons—and, sadly I say it, even more outside the churches whom bitterness at racial inconsistency of white Christians had soured into a silent disbelief of all religion. In either class she would have found no trouble in reaching a heart which could enter into all the agony of her own trial and bitter grief. Nor am I so sure, if she had followed her first gushing impulse to go South and "elevate" the race with whom she had discovered her relationship, that she would have found even them so ready to receive her condescending patronage.

There are numerous other inadvertent misrepresentations in the book—such as supposing that colored people voluntarily and deliberately prefer to keep to themselves in all public places and that from choice "they have their own neighborhoods, their own churches, their own amusements, their own resorts,"—the intimation that there is a "*black* voice," a black character, easy, irresponsible and fond of what is soft and pleasant, a black ideal of art and a black barbaric taste in color, a black affinity—so that in some occult and dreadful way one, only one-sixteenth related and totally foreign by education and environment, can still feel that one-sixteenth race calling her more loudly than the fifteen-sixteenths. I wish to do Mr. Howells the justice to admit, however, that one feels his blunders to be wholly unintentional and due to the fact that he has studied his subject merely from the outside. With all his matchless powers as a novelist, not even he can yet "think himself imaginatively" into the colored man's place.

To my mind the quaintest and truest little bit of portraiture from low-life that I have read in a long time is the little story that appeared last winter in the Harpers, of the "*Widder Johnsing and how she caught the preacher.*" It is told with naive impersonality and appreciative humor, and is quite equal, I think, both in subject and treatment to the best of Mrs. Stowe's New England dialect stories. It is idyllic in its charming simplicity and naturalness, and delightfully fresh in its sparkling wit and delicious humor. We do not resent such pictures as this of our lowly folk—such a homely and honest

"Pomegranate, which, if cut deep down the middle,
  Shows a heart within blood tinctured of a *veined humanity,*"

is always sweet to the taste and dear to the heart, however plain and humble the setting.

A longer and more elaborate work, Harold, published anonymously, comes properly in our group second, the didactic novel. It gives the picture of a black Englishman cultured and refined, brought in painful contact with American,—or rather *un-American*, color prejudice. The point of the book seems to be to show that education for the black man is a curse, since it increases his sensitiveness to the indignities he must suffer in consequence of white barbarity. The author makes Harold, after a futile struggle against American inequalities, disappear into the jungles of Africa, "there to wed a dusky savage," at the last cursing the day he had ever suspected a broader light or known a higher aspiration; a conclusion which, to my mind, is a most illogical one. If the cultivated black man cannot endure the white man's barbarity—the cure, it seems to me, would be to cultivate the white man. Civilize both, then each will know what is due from man to man, and that reduces at once to a minimum the friction of their contact.

In the same rank as Harold belongs that improbability of improbabilities, Doctor Huguet, by the arch-sensationalist, Ignatius Donelly. As its purpose is evidently good, I shall not undertake to review the book. Suffice it to say the plot hinges on the exchange of soul between the body of a black chicken-thief and that of a cultivated white gentleman, and sets forth the indignities and wrongs to which the cultured soul, with all its past of refinement and learning, has to submit in consequence of its change of cuticle. The book is an able protest against that snobbishness which elevates complexion into a touchstone of aristocracy and makes the pigment cells of a man's skin his badge of nobility regardless of the foulness or purity of the soul within; the only adverse criticism from the colored man's point of view being the selection of a chicken thief as his typical black man; but on the principle of antitheses this may have been artistically necessary.

I shall pass next to what I consider the most significant contribution to this subject for the last ten years—a poem by Maurice Thompson in the New York Independent for January 21, 1892, entitled *A Voodoo Prophecy*. From beginning to end it is full of ghoulish imagery and fine poetic madness. Here are a few stanzas of it:

> "I am the prophet of the dusky race,
>   The poet of wild Africa. Behold,
> The midnight vision brooding in my face!
>   Come near me,
>   And hear me,
>   While from my lips the words of Fate are told.
>
> A black and terrible memory masters me,
>   The shadow and the substance of deep wrong;
> You know the past, hear now what is to be:
>   From the midnight land,
>   Over sea and sand,
>   From the green jungle, hear my Voodoo-song:
>
> A tropic heat is in my bubbling veins,
>   Quintessence of all savagery is mine,
> The lust of ages ripens in my reins,
>   And burns
>   And yearns,
>   Like venom-sap within a noxious vine.
>
> Was I a heathen? Ay, I was—am still
>   A fetich worshipper; but I was free
> To loiter or to wander at my will,
>   To leap and dance,

          To hurl my lance,
And breathe the air of savage liberty.

You drew me to a higher life, you say;
    Ah, drove me, with the lash of slavery!
Am I unmindful? Every cursed day
                Of pain
                And chain
Roars like a torrent in my memory.

You make my manhood whole with 'equal rights!'
    Poor empty words! Dream you I honor them?—
I who have stood on Freedom's wildest hights?
                My Africa,
                I see the day
When none dare touch thy garment's lowest hem.

You cannot make me love you with your whine
    Of fine repentance. Veil your pallid face
In presence of the shame that mantles mine;
                Stand
                At command
Of the black prophet of the Negro race!

I hate you, and I live to nurse my hate,
    Remembering when you plied the slaver's trade
In my dear land . . . How patiently I wait
                The day,
                Not far away,
When all your pride shall shrivel up and fade.

Yea, all your whiteness darken under me!
    Darken and be jaundiced, and your blood
Take in dread humors from my savagery,
                Until
                Your will
Lapse into mine and seal my masterhood.

You, seed of Abel, proud of your descent,
    And arrogant, because your cheeks are fair,

Within my loins an inky curse is pent,
                    To flood
                    Your blood
        And stain your skin and crisp your golden hair.

As you have done by me, so will I do
        By all the generations of your race;
Your snowy limbs, your blood's patrician blue
                    Shall be
                    Tainted by me,
        And I will set my seal upon your face!

Yea, I will dash my blackness down your veins,
        And through your nerves my sensuousness I'll fling;
Your lips, your eyes, shall bear the musty stains
                    Of Congo kisses,
                    While shrieks and hisses
        Shall blend into the savage songs I sing!

Your temples will I break, your fountains fill,
        Your cities raze, your fields to deserts turn;
My heathen fires shall shine on every hill,
                    And wild beasts roam,
                    Where stands your home;—
        Even the wind your hated dust shall spurn.

I will absorb your very life in me,
        And mold you to the shape of my desire;
Back through the cycles of all cruelty
                    I will swing you,
                    And wring you,
        And roast you in my passions' hottest fire.

You, North and South, you, East and West,
        Shall drink the cup your fathers gave to me;
My back still burns, I bare my bleeding breast,
                    I set my face,
                    My limbs I brace,
        To make the long, strong fight for mastery.

My serpent fetich lolls its withered lip
    And bares its shining fangs at thought of this:
I scarce can hold the monster in my grip.
            So strong is he,
            So eagerly
He leaps to meet my precious prophecies.

Hark for the coming of my countless host,
    Watch for my banner over land and sea.
The ancient power of vengeance is not lost!
            Lo! on the sky
            The fire-clouds fly,
And strangely moans the windy, weltering sea."

Now this would be poetry if it were only truthful. Simple and sensuous it surely is, but it lacks the third requisite—truth. The Negro is utterly incapable of such vindictiveness. Such concentrated venom might be distilled in the cold Saxon, writhing and chafing under oppression and repression such as the Negro in America has suffered and is suffering. But the black man is in real life only too glad to accept the olive branch of reconciliation. He merely asks to be let alone. To be allowed to pursue his destiny as a free man and an American citizen, to rear and educate his children in peace, to engage in art, science, trades or industries according to his ability,— and *to go to the wall if he fail.* He is willing, if I understand him, to let bygones be bygones. He does not even demand satisfaction for the centuries of his ancestors' unpaid labor. He asks neither pension, nor dole nor back salaries; but is willing to start from the bottom, all helpless and unprovided for as he is, with absolutely nothing as his stock in trade, with no capital, in a country developed, enriched, and made to blossom through his father's "sweat and toil,"—with none of the accumulations of ancestors' labors, with no education or moral training for the duties and responsibilities of freedom; nay, with every power, mental, moral, and physical, emasculated by a debasing slavery—he is willing, even glad to take his place in the lists alongside his oppressors, who have had every advantage, to be tried with them by their own standards, and to ask no quarter from them or high Heaven to palliate or excuse the ignominy of a defeat.

The Voodoo Prophecy has no interest then as a picture of the black, but merely as a revelation of the white man. Maurice

Thompson in penning this portrait of the Negro, has, unconsciously
it may be, laid bare his own soul—its secret dread and horrible fear.
And this, it seems to me, is the key to the Southern situation, the
explanation of the apparent heartlessness and cruelty of some, and the
stolid indifference to atrocity on the part of others, before which so
many of us have stood paralyzed in dumb dismay. The Southerner is
not a cold-blooded villain. Those of us who have studied the genus
in its native habitat can testify that his impulses are generous and
kindly, and that while the South presents a solid phalanx of iron
resistance to the Negro's advancement, still as individuals to individuals they are warm-hearted and often even tender. And just here
is the difference between the Southerner and his more philosophical,
less sentimental Northern brother. The latter in an abstract metaphysical way rather wants you to have all the rights that belong to
you. He thinks it better for the country, better for him that justice,
universal justice be done. But he doesn't care to have the blacks, in
the concrete, too near him. He doesn't know them and doesn't want
to know them. He really can't understand how the Southerner could
have let those little cubs get so close to him as they did in the old
days—nursing from the same bottle and feeding at the same breast.

To the Southerner, on the other hand, race antipathy and color-
phobia *as such* does not exist. Personally, there is hardly a man of
them but knows, and has known from childhood, some black fellow whom he loves as dearly as if he were white, whom he regards
as indispensable to his own pleasures, and for whom he would
break every commandment in the decalogue to save him from any
general disaster. But our Bourbon seems utterly incapable of generalizing his few ideas. He would die for A or B, but suddenly
becomes utterly impervious to every principle of logic when you
ask for the simple golden rule to be applied to the class of which A
or B is one. Another fact strikes me as curious. A Southern white
man's regard for his black friend varies in inverse ratio to the real
distance between them in education and refinement. Puck expresses
it—"I can get on a great deal better with a nigger than I can with
a Negro." And Mr. Douglass puts it: "Let a colored man be out at
elbows and toes and half way into the gutter and there is no prejudice against him; but let him respect himself and be a man and
Southern whites can't abide to ride in the same car with him."

Why this anomaly? Is it pride? Ordinarily, congeniality increases
with similarity in taste and manners. Is it antipathy to color? It does

not exist. The explanation is the white man's dread dimly shadowed out in this Voodoo Prophecy of Maurice Thompson, and fed and inspired by such books as Minden Armais and a few wild theorizers who have nothing better to do with their time than spend it advocating the fusion of races as a plausible and expedient policy. Now I believe there are two ideas which master the Southern white man and incense him against the black race. On this point he is a monomaniac. In the face of this feeling he would not admit he was convinced of the axioms of Geometry. The one is personal and present, the fear of Negro political domination. The other is for his posterity—the future horror of being lost as a race in this virile and vigorous black race. Relieve him of this nightmare and he becomes "as gentle as the sucking dove." With that dread delusion maddening him he would drive his sword to the hilt in the tender breast of his darling child, did he fancy that through her the curse would come.

Now argument is almost supersensible with a monomaniac. What is most needed is a sedative for the excited nerves, and then a mental tonic to stimulate the power of clear perception and truthful cerebration. The Southern patient needs to be brought to see, by the careful and cautious injection of cold facts and by the presentation of well selected object lessons that so far as concerns his first named horror of black supremacy politically, the usual safeguards of democracy are in the hands of intelligence and wealth in the South as elsewhere. The weapons of fair argument and persuasion, the precautionary bulwark of education and justice, the unimpeachable supremacy and insuperable advantage of intelligence and discipline over mere numbers—are all in his reach. It is to his interest to help make the black peasant an intelligent and self-respecting citizen. No section can thrive under the incubus of an illiterate, impoverished, cheerless and hopeless peasantry. Let the South once address herself in good faith to the improvement of the condition of her laboring classes, let her give but a tithe of the care and attention which are bestowed in the North on its mercurial and inflammable importations, let her show but the disposition in her relative poverty merely to utter the benediction, *Be ye warmed and fed and educated*, even while she herself has not the wherewithal to emulate the Pullman villages and the Carnegie munificence, let her but give him a fair wage and an honest reckoning and a kindly God-speed,—and she will find herself in possession of the most tractable laborer, the most faithful and reliable henchman, the most invaluable co-operator and friendly vassal of which this or any country can boast.

So far as regards the really less sane idea that amicable relations subsisting between the races may promote their ultimate blending and loss of identity, it hardly seems necessary to refute it. Blending of races in the aggregate is simply an unthinkable thought, and the union of individuals can never fall out by accident or haphazard. There must be the deliberate wish and intention on each side; and the average black man in this country is as anxious to preserve his identity and transmit his type as is the average white man. In any case, hybridity is in no sense dependent on sectional or national amity. Oppression and outrage are not the means to chain the affections. Cupid, who knows no bolt or bars, is more wont to be stimulated with romantic sympathy towards a forbidden object unjustly persecuted. The sensible course is to remove those silly and unjust barriers which protect nothing and merely call attention to the possibilities of law-breaking, and depend instead on religion and common sense to guide, control and direct in the paths of purity and right reason.

The froth and foam, the sticks and debris at the watertop may have an uncertain movement, but as deep calleth unto deep the mighty ocean swell is always true to the tides; and whatever the fluctuations along the ragged edge between the races, the home instinct is sufficiently strong with each to hold the great mass true to its attractions. If Maurice Thompson's nightmare vision is sincere on his part, then, it has no objective reality; 'tis merely a hideous phantasm bred of his own fevered and jaundiced senses; if he does not believe in it himself, it was most unkind and uncalled for to publish abroad such inflaming and irritating fabrications.

After this cursory glance at a few contributions which have peculiarly emphasized one phase of our literature during the last decade or two, I am brought to the conclusion that an authentic portrait, at once æsthetic and true to life, presenting the black man as a free American citizen, not the humble slave of *Uncle Tom's Cabin*—but the *man*, divinely struggling and aspiring yet tragically warped and distorted by the adverse winds of circumstance, has not yet been painted. It is my opinion that the canvas awaits the brush of the colored man himself. It is a pathetic—a fearful arraignment of America's conditions of life, that instead of that enrichment from the years and days, the summers and springs under which, as Browning says,

"The flowers turn double and the leaves turn flowers,"—

the black man's native and original flowers have in this country been all hardened and sharpened into thorns and spurs. In literature we have no artists for art's sake. Albery A. Whitman in *"Twasinta's Seminoles"* and *"Not a Man and Yet a Man"* is almost the only poet who has attempted a more sustained note than the lyrics of Mrs. Harper, and even that note is almost a wail.

The fact is, a sense of freedom in mind as well as in body is necessary to the appreciative and inspiring pursuit of the beautiful. A bird cannot warble out his fullest and most joyous notes while the wires of his cage are pricking and cramping him at every heart beat. His tones become only the shrill and poignant protest of rage and despair. And so the black man's vexations and chafing environment, even since his physical emancipation has given him speech, has goaded him into the eloquence and fire of oratory rather than the genial warmth and cheery glow of either poetry or romance. And pity 'tis, 'tis true. A race that has produced for America the only folk-lore and folk songs of native growth, a race which has grown the most original and unique assemblage of fable and myth to be found on the continent, a race which has suggested and inspired almost the only distinctive American note which could chain the attention and charm the ear of the outside world—has as yet found no mouthpiece of its own to unify and perpetuate its wondrous whisperings—no painter-poet to distil in the alembic of his own imagination the gorgeous dyes, the luxuriant juices of this rich and tropical vegetation. It was the glory of Chaucer that he justified the English language to itself—that he took the homely and hitherto despised Saxon elements and ideas, and lovingly wove them into an artistic product which even Norman conceit and uppishness might be glad to acknowledge and imitate. The only man who is doing the same for Negro folk-lore is one not to the manner born. Joel Chandler Harris has made himself rich and famous by simply standing around among the black railroad hands and cotton pickers of the South and compiling the simple and dramatic dialogues which fall from their lips. What I hope to see before I die is a black man honestly and appreciatively portraying both the Negro as he is, and the white man, occasionally, as seen from the Negro's standpoint.

There is an old proverb "The devil is always painted *black*—by white painters." And what is needed, perhaps, to reverse the picture of the lordly man slaying the lion, is for the lion to turn painter.

Then too we need the calm clear judgment of ourselves and of others born of a disenchantment similar to that of a little girl I know in the South, who was once being laboriously held up over the shoulders of a surging throng to catch her first glimpse of a real live president. "Why Nunny," she cried half reproachfully, as she strained her little neck to see—"*It's nuffin but a man!*"

When we have been sized up and written down by others, we need not feel that the last word is said and the oracles sealed. "It's nuffin but a man." And there are many gifts the giftie may gie us, far better than seeing ourselves as others see us—and one is that of Bion's maxim "*Know Thyself.*" Keep true to your own ideals. Be not ashamed of what is homely and your own. Speak out and speak honestly. Be true to yourself and to the message God and Nature meant you to deliver. The young David cannot fight in Saul's unwieldy armor. Let him simply therefore gird his loins, take up his own parable and tell this would-be great American nation "*A chile's amang ye takin' notes;*" and when men act the part of cowards or wild beasts, this great silent but open-eyed constituency has a standard by which they are being tried. Know thyself, and know those around at their true weight of solid intrinsic manhood without being dazzled by the fact that littleness of soul is often gilded with wealth, power and intellect. There can be no nobility but that of soul, and no catalogue of adventitious circumstances can wipe out the stain or palliate the meanness of inflicting one ruthless, cruel wrong. 'Tis not only safer, but nobler, grander, diviner,

> "To be that which we destroy
> Than, by destruction, dwell in doubtful joy."

With this platform to stand on we can with clear eye weigh what is written and estimate what is done and ourselves paint what is true with the calm spirit of those who know their cause is right and who believe there is a God who judgeth the nations.

WHAT ARE WE WORTH?

I ONCE HEARD Henry Ward Beecher make this remark: "Were Africa and the Africans to sink to-morrow, how much poorer would the world be? A little less gold and ivory, a little less coffee, a considerable ripple, perhaps, where the Atlantic and Indian Oceans would come together—that is all; not a poem, not an invention, not a piece of art would be missed from the world."

This is not a flattering statement; but then we do not want flattery if seeing ourselves as others see us is to help us in fulfilling the higher order, "know thyself." The world is often called cold and hard. I don't know much about that; but of one thing I am sure, it is intensely practical. Waves of sentiment or prejudice may blur its old eyes for a little while but you are sure to have your bill presented first or last with the inexorable "How much owest thou?" What have you produced, what consumed? What is your real value in the world's economy? What do you give to the world over and above what you have cost? What would be missed had you never lived? What are you worth? What of actual value would go down with you if you were sunk into the ocean or buried by an earthquake to-morrow? Show up your cash account and your balance sheet. In the final reckoning do you belong on the debit or the credit side of the account? according to a fair and square, an impartial and practical reckoning. It is by this standard that society estimates individuals; and by this standard finally and inevitably the world will measure and judge nations and races.

It may not be unprofitable then for us to address ourselves to the task of casting up our account and carefully overhauling our books. It may be well to remember at the outset that the operation is purely a mathematical one and allows no room for sentiment. The good housewife's pet chicken which she took when first hatched, fed from her own hand and fondled on her bosom as lovingly as if it were a babe, is worth no more (for all the affection and care lavished

111

on it) when sold in the shambles: and that never-to-be-forgotten black hen that stole into the parlor, flew upon the mantel looking for a nest among those handsome curios, smashed the sèvers vases and picked the buds from the lovely tea rose—so exasperatingly that the good woman could never again endure the sight of her—this ill-fated bird is worth no less. There are sections of this country in which the very name of the Negro, even in homeopathic doses, stirs up such a storm of feeling that men fairly grow wild and are unfit to discuss the simplest principles of life and conduct where the colored man is concerned; and you would think it necessary for the Ethiopian actually to change his skin before there can be any harmonious living or lucid thinking: there are a few nooks and crannies, on the other hand, in another quarter of the same country, in which that name embodies an idealized theory and a benevolent sentiment; and the black man (the blacker the better) is the petted nursling, the haloed idea, the foregone conclusion. In these Arcadias, it is as good capital as pushing selfishness and aspiring mediocrity need ask, to be advertised as one of the oppressed race and probably born a slave.

But after all sentiment, whether adverse or favorable, is ephemeral. Ever shifting and unreliable, it can never be counted in estimating values. The sentiments of youth are outgrown in age, and we like to-day what we despised or were indifferent to yesterday. Nine-tenths of the mis-called color prejudice or race prejudice in this country is mere sentiment governed by the association of ideas. It is not color prejudice at all. The color of a man's face *per se* has no more to do with his worthiness and companionableness than the color of his eyes or the shades of his hair. You admire the one or think the other more beautiful to rest the gaze upon. But every one with brains knows and must admit that he must look deeper than this for the man. Mrs. Livermore once said in my hearing: "It is not that the Negro is black; Spaniards, Portuguese, East Indians, enter our parlors, sup at our tables, and, if they have a sufficiently long bank account, they may marry our daughters: but the Negro is weak—and we don't like weakness."

Now this dislike it is useless to inveigh against and folly to rail at. We share it ourselves and often carry it to a more unjustifiable extent. For as a rule the narrower the mind and the more circumscribed the experience, the greater will be the exaggeration of accidents over substance, and of circumstance over soul. It does no good to argue with the poor sea-sick wretch who, even on land after the voyage, is nauseated by the sight of clear spring water. In vain you show the unreason of the feeling. This, you explain, is a different time, a different place, a different stage of progress in the circulation of waters. That was salt, this is fresh, and so on. You might as well be presenting syllogisms to Ætna. "Yes, my dear Fellow," he cries, "You talk admirably; but you don't know how I feel. You don't know how sick I was on that nasty ship!" And so your rhetoric cannot annihilate the association of ideas. He feels; *you know.* But he will outgrow his feeling,—and you are content to wait.

Just as impervious to reason is the man who is dominated by the sentiment of race prejudice. You can only consign him to the fatherly hand of Time; and pray that your own mental sight be not thus obscured and your judgment warped in your endeavors to be just and true.

Sentiment and cant, then, both being ruled out, let us try to study our subject as the world finally reckons it—not certain crevices and crannies of the earth, but the cool, practical, business-like world. What are we worth? not in Georgia nor in Massachusetts; not to our brothers and sisters and cousins and aunts, every one of whom would unhesitatingly declare us worth a great gold-lump; nor to the exasperated neighbor over the way who would be just as ready, perhaps, to write us down a most unmitigated nuisance. But what do we represent to the world? What is our market value. Are we a positive and additive quantity or a negative factor in the world's elements. What have we cost and what do we come to?

The calculation may be made in the same way and on the same principle that we would estimate the value of any commodity on the market. Men are not very unlike watches. We might estimate first the cost of material—is it gold or silver or alloy, solid or plated, jewelled or sham paste. Settle the relative value of your raw material, and next you want to calculate how much this value has been enhanced by labor, the delicacy and fineness, the honesty and thoroughness of the workmanship; then the utility and beauty of the product and its adaptability to the end and purpose of its manufacture; and lastly is there a demand in the market for such an article. Does it meet a want, *will it go* and *go right?* Is it durable and reliable. How often do you have to wind it before it runs down, how often repair it. Does it keep good time and require but little watching and looking after. And there is no radical difference, after all, between the world's way of estimating men and our usual way of valuing watches. In both the fundamental item is the question of material, and then the refining and enhancement of that material through labor, and so on through the list.

What then can we say for our raw material?

Again I must preface an apology for anything unpalatable in our menu. I promised, you remember, to leave out the sentiment—you may stir it in afterwards, mixing thoroughly according to taste. We must discuss facts, candidly and bluntly, without rhetoric or cant if we would have a clear light on our problem.

Now whatever notions we may indulge on the theory of evolution and the laws of atavism or heredity, all concede that no individual character receives its raw material newly created and independent of the rock from whence it was hewn. No life is bound up within the period of its conscious existence. No personality dates its origin from its birthday. The elements that are twisted into the cord did not begin their formation when first the tiny thread became visible in the great warp and filling of humanity. When first we saw the light many of the threads undoubtedly were spun and the color and fineness of the weft determined. The materials that go to make the man, the probabilities of his character and activities, the conditions and circumstances of his growth, and his quantum of resistance and mastery are the resultant of forces which have been accumulating and gathering momentum for generations. So that, as one tersely expresses it, in order to reform a man, you must begin with his great grandmother.

A few years ago a certain social scientist was struck by a remarkable coincidence in the name of a number of convicts in the State prison of New York. There were found thirty-five or forty men, of the same name with but slight modification in the spelling, all convicted of crimes similar in character. Looking into the matter, he traced them every one back to one woman of inferior character who had come from England in one of the first colonial ships. *And that woman had been a convict and charged with pretty nearly the same crime.*

Rightly to estimate our material, then, it is necessary to go back of the twenty or thirty years during which we have been in possession, and find out the nature of the soil in which it has been forming and growing.

There is or used to be in England a system of entail by which a lot of land was fixed to a family and its posterity forever, passing always on the death of the father to his eldest son. A man may mis-use or abuse, he may impoverish, mortgage, sterilize, eliminate every element of value—but he can never sell. He may cut down every tree, burn every fence and house, abstract by careless tillage, or by no tillage, every nutritive element from the soil, encumber it to two or three times its value and destroy forever its beauty and fertility—but he can never rid himself of it. That land with all its encumbrances and liabilities, its barrenness and squalidness, its pov-erty and its degradation is inexorably, inevitably, inalienably his; and like a shattered and debased personality it haunts him wherever he goes. An heir coming into an estate is thus often poorer than if he had no inheritance. He is chained to a life long possession of debt, toil, responsibility, often disgrace. Happier were it for him if he could begin life with nothing—an isolated but free man with no capital but his possibilities, with no past and no pedigree. And so it often is with men. These bodies of ours often come to us mortgaged to their full value by the extravagance, self-indulgence, sensuality of some ancestor. Some man, generations back, has encumbered his estate for strong drink, his descendants coming into that estate have the mortgage to pay off, principal and interest. Another cut down the fences of character by debauchery and vice,—and these have to ward off attacks of the enemy without bulwarks or embattlements. They have burnt their houses of purity and integrity, have rendered the soil poor and unproductive by extravagance and folly,—and the children have to shiver amid the storms of passion and feed on husks till they can build for themselves a shelter and fertilize their farms. Not very valuable estates, you will say. Well, no,—nothing to boast of, perhaps. But an energetic heir can often pay off some of the liabilities and leave the estate to his children less involved than when he received it. At least he can arrest the work of destruction and see to it that no further encumbrances are added through his folly and mismanagement.

In estimating the value of our material, therefore, it is plain that we must look into the deeds of our estates and ferret out their his-tory. The task is an individual one, as likewise its application. Certainly the original timber as it came from the African forests was good enough. No race of heathen are more noted for honesty and chastity than are the tribes of Africa. For one of their women to violate the laws of purity is a crime punishable with death; and so strictly honest are they, it is said, that they are wont to leave their commodities at the place of exchange and go about their business. The buyer coming up takes what he wishes to purchase and leaves its equivalent in barter or money. A returned missionary tells the story that certain European traders, when at a loss as to the safe keeping of their wares, were told by a native chief, "Oh just lay them down there. *They are perfectly safe, there are no Christians here.*"

Whatever may be said of its beauty, then, the black side of the stream with us is pretty pure, and has no cause to blush for its honesty and integrity. From the nature of the case the infusions of white blood that have come in many instances to the black race in this country are not the best that race afforded. And if anything further is needed to account for racial irregularities—the warping and shrinking, the knotting and cracking of the sturdy old timber, the two hundred and fifty years of training here are quite sufficient to explain all. I have often thought, since coming in closer contact with the Puritan element in America, what a different planing and shaping this timber might have received under their hands!

As I compare the Puritan's sound, substantial, sanctified common sense with the Feudal froth and foam of the South; the Puritan's liberal, democratic, ethical and at the same time calculating, economical, stick-to-ative and go-ahead-ative spirit,—with the free and easy lavishness, the aristocratic notions of caste and class distinctions, the pliable consciences and unbending social bars amid which I was reared;—I have wished that it might have been ordered that as my race had to serve a term of bondage it might have been under the discipline of the successors of Cromwell and Milton, rather than under the training and example of the luxurious cavaliers. There is no doubt that the past two hundred and fifty years of working up the material we now inherit, has depreciated rather than enhanced its value. We find in it the foolish ideas of aristocracy founded on anything else than a moral claim; we find the contempt for manual labor and the horror of horny palms, the love of lavish expenditure and costly display, and—alas, that we must own it—the laxness of morals and easy-going consciences inherited and imitated from the old English gentry of the reigns of Charles and Anne. But to know our faults is one step toward correcting them, and there are, I trust, no flaws in this first element of value, *material*, which may not be planed and scraped and sand-papered out by diligent and strenuous effort. One thing is certain, the flaws that are simply ingrained in the timber are not our responsibility. A man is to be praised primarily not for having inherited fine tools and faultless materials but for making the most of the stuff he has, and doing his best in spite of disadvantages and poor material. The individual is responsible, not for what he has not, but for what he has; and the vital part for us after all depends on the use we make of our material.

Many a passable article has by diligent workmanship been made even from inferior material. And this brings us to our second item of value—Labor.

This is a most important item. It would seem sometimes that it is labor that creates all value. A gold mine is worth no more than common clay till it is worked. The simple element of labor bestowed on iron, the cheapest and commonest of metals, multiplies its value four hundred thousand times, making it worth sixty-five times its weight in gold, *e. g.:*

A pound of good iron is worth about .... 4 cts.
A pound of inch screws $1.00
A pound of steel wire from.................... $3.00 to $7.00
A pound of sewing needles........................ $14.00
A pound of fish hooks from .... $20 00 to $50.00
A pound of jewel screws for watches $3,500.00
A pound of hair springs for watches $16,000.00
While a pound of fine gold in standard
    coin is worth only about........................ $248.00

Now it is the same fundamental material in the hair springs valued at $16,000.00 which was sold in the rough at 4 cts. per pound. It is labor that has thus enhanced its value. Now let us see if there is a parallel rise of value in the material of which men are made.

No animal, the scientists tell us, is in infancy so utterly helpless, so completely destitute of the means of independent existence, so entirely worthless in itself as the world estimates values, as is man. The chick just out of the shell can pick up its own food and run away from approaching danger. Touch a snapping turtle just a moment after its birth, and it will bite at you. Cut off its head and it will still bite. Break open the egg of the young and the vivacious little creature will, even in the embryo, try to fight for its rights and maintain its independence. But the human babe can for weeks and months, do nothing but cry and feed and fear. It is a constant drain on the capital of its parents, both physically and mentally. It is to be fed, and worked for, and sheltered and protected. It cannot even defend itself against a draft of wind.

What is it worth? Unsentimentally and honestly,—it is worth just as much as a leak is worth to a ship, or what the mistletoe is worth to the oak. He is a parasite, a thief, a destroyer of values. He thrives at another's expense, and filches from that other every atom of his own existence. The infatuated mother, it is true, would not sell him, she will tell you, for his weight in gold; but that is sentiment—not business. Besides, there is no danger of her having the chance to make such a bargain. No one will ever tempt her with any such offer. The world knows too well what an outlay of time and money and labor must be made before he is worth even his weight in ashes. His present worth no one would accept even as a gift—and it is only the prospect of future development of worth that could induce any one, save that mother, to take up the burden. What an expenditure of toil and care, of heart power and brain power, what planning, what working, what feeding, what enriching, what sowing and sinking of values before one can tell whether the harvest is worth the output. Yet, how gladly does the mother pour out her strength and vitality, her energy, her life that the little bankrupt may store up capital for its own use. How anxiously does she hang over the lumpish little organism to catch the first awakening of a soul. And when the chubby little hands begin to swing consciously before the snapping eyes, and the great toe is caught and tugged towards the open mouth, when the little pink fists for the first time linger caressingly on her cheek and breast, and the wide open eyes say distinctly "I know you, I love you,"—how she strains him to her bosom as her whole soul goes out to this newly found intelligence in the impassioned cry of Carlyle: "*Whence—and Oh Heavens, whither!*"

> "How poor, how rich, how abject, how august,
> How complicate, how wonderful is man!"

It is labor, development, training, careful, patient, painful, diligent toil that must span the gulf between this vegetating life germ (now worth nothing but toil and care and trouble, and living purely at the expense of another)—and that future consummation in which "the elements are so mixed that Nature can stand up and say to all the world, '*This is a man.*'"

It is a heavy investment, requires a large outlay of money on long time and large risk, no end of labor, skill, pains. Education is the word that covers it all—the working up of this raw material and fitting it into the world's work to supply the world's need—the manufacture of men and women for the markets of the world. But there is no other labor which so creates value. The value of the well developed man has been enhanced far more by the labor bestowed than is the iron in the watch springs. The value of the raw material was far below zero to begin with; but this "quintessence of dust" has become, *through labor*, "the beauty of the world, the paragon of animals,—noble in reason and infinite in faculty!"

What a piece of work, indeed!

Education, then, is the safest and richest investment possible to man. It pays the largest dividends and gives the grandest possible product to the world—a man. The demand is always greater than the supply—and the world pays well for what it prizes.

Now what sort of workmanship are we putting on our raw material. What are we doing for education? The man-factories among our people make, I think, a fairly good showing. Figures are encouraging things to deal with, and too they represent something tangible in casting up our accounts. There are now 25,530 colored schools in the United States with 1,353,352 pupils; the colored people hold in landed property for churches and schools $25,000,000. 2,500,000 colored children have learned to read and most of these to write also. 22,956 colored men and women are teaching in these schools. There are sixty-six academies and high schools and one hundred and fifty schools for advanced education taught by colored teachers, together with seven colleges administered by colored presidents and faculties. There are now one thousand college bred Negro ministers in the country, 250 lawyers, 749 physicians; while, according to Dr. Rankin, there are 247 colored students preparing themselves in the universities of Europe.

The African Methodists alone, representing the unassisted effort of the colored people for self-development, have founded thirty-eight institutes and colleges, with landed property valued at $502,650, and 134 teachers supported entirely by the self denying effort of the colored people themselves.

This looks like an attempt, to say the least, to do the best we can with our material. One feels there has not been much shirking here; the workmanship may be crude sometimes, when measured by more finished standards,—but they have done what they could; in their poverty and inexperience, through self denial and persever-ance, they are struggling upward toward the light.

There is another item to be taken into account in estimating the value of a product, to which we must give just a thought in passing, *i.e.*, the necessary waste of material in the making.

The Sultan of Turkey once sent to China to procure a *fac simile* of some elegant plates he had had, all of which were now broken but one and that, unfortunately, was cracked. He sent this one as a pattern and requested that the set be renewed exactly like the for-mer ones. He was surprised on receiving the plates to note the fabulous sum charged for them,—but the Celestial explained that the cost was greatly increased by having *to put in the crack*,—so many had been lost in the making.

The anecdote is not my own, but it suggests a thought that may be useful to us and I borrow it for that purpose. They tell us that the waste of material is greater in making colored men and women than in the case of others—that a larger percentage of our children die under twenty-one years of age, especially in large cities, and that a larger number who reach that age and beyond, are to be classed among the world's invalids and paupers. According to the census of 1880 the average death rate throughout the country was, among the whites 14.74 per 1000; among colored 17.28 per 1000: the highest among whites being in New Mexico, 22.04, lowest in Arizona, 7.91 per 1000. Among colored, the mortality ranges from 35.25 in the District of Columbia where it is the highest, to 1.89 in Arizona, the lowest.

For 1889 the relative death-rate of the two races in the District of Columbia was: whites, 15.96 per 1000; colored, 30.48, about dou-ble. In 1888 they stood 18+ to 30+; in 1886 and '87, about 17 to 31; in '85 and '86, 17 to 32. Especially noticeable is the difference in the mortality of children. This is simply alarming. The report for 1889 shows that out of the 5,152 deaths occurring in the District of Columbia during that year, 634 were white infants under one year old, while 834, an excess of 200, within the same limits were colored. Yet the white population of the District outnumbers the colored two to one. The Health Commissioner, in his report for that year, says: "This material difference in mortality may be charged to a great extent to the massing of colored people in alleys and unhealthy parts of the city and to their unsanitary surroundings: while there is no

doubt that a very large proportion of these children die in consequence of being fed improper and unhealthy food, especially cheap
and badly prepared condensed milk, and cow's milk which has been
allowed to stand to the point of acidity after having been kept in ves-
sels badly or unskillfully cleaned." And he adds, "if the general statistics of infant mortality seem astounding to the public, the cause can
most frequently be found in the reprehensible custom of committing
little impoverished waifs to hired nurses and foul feeding bottles
rather than allow them the food that nature has provided."

Now all this unquestionably represents a most wanton and fla-
grant *waste* of valuable material. By sapping out the possibilities of
a healthy and vigorous existence it is deliberately and flagitiously
breeding and multiplying paupers, criminals, idiots, drunkards,
imbeciles and lunatics to infest and tax the commonwealth. The
number spoiled in the making necessarily adds to the cost of those
who survive. It is like the Sultan's cracked dinner-plates. It is no use
to go into hysterics and explode in Ciceronian phillippics against
life insurance companies for refusing to insure or charging a higher
premium for colored policies. With them it is simply a question of
dollars and cents. What are you worth? What are your chances, and
what does it cost to take your risks in the aggregate? If thirty-five
colored persons out of every thousand are, from any cause whatever, lost in the making, the remaining nine hundred and sixty-five
will have to share the loss among them. This is an unavoidable law.
No man can dissociate himself from his kind. The colored gentleman who keeps his horses, fares sumptuously, and lives in luxury is
made to feel the death gasps of every squalid denizen of the alley
and poor-house. It is God's own precaution to temper our self-
seeking by binding our sympathies and interests indissolubly with
the helpless and the wretched.

What our men of means need to do, then, is to devote their
money, their enlightened interest, their careful attention to the
improvement of sanitation among the poor. Let some of those who
can command real estate in healthful localities build sweet and clean
and wholesome tenements *on streets* and rent them at reasonable rates
to the worthy poor who are at present forced into association with
the vileness and foulness of alleys and filthy courts by the unfeeling
discrimination of white dealers. Let some colored capitalists buy up
a few of those immense estates in the South, divide them into single
farms with neat, cheery, well-ventilated, healthsome cottages to be

rented to the colored tenants who are toiling all these weary years in the one-room log but, like their own cheerless mules—just to fodder themselves.

In cities, low priced houses on streets are almost uniformly kept for the white poor. I know of numerous houses in Washington the rent of which is no dearer than colored people are paying in alleys—but the advertisement says, "not rented to colored people." If the presence of a colored tenant in a neighborhood causes property to depreciate, it may be a question of sentiment,—it must be a question of business. The former it is superfluous to inveigh against or even to take cognizance of. It is possibly subject to enlightenment, and probably a sickness not unto death. But the practical reason underlying it is directly our concern and should command our energetic consideration. It is largely a question of what are we worth—and as such, subject to our immediate responsibility and amendment. If improvement is possible, if it is in our power to render ourselves *valuable* to a community or neighborhood, it should be the work of the earnest and able men and women among us, the moral physicians and reformers, to devise and apply a remedy. Sure it is that the burden rests on all till the deliverance comes. The richest and most highly favored cannot afford to be indifferent or to rest quietly complacent.

In rural districts, the relative mortality of colored people is not so excessive, still the poverty and destitution, the apparent dearth of accumulation notwithstanding ceaseless drudging toil is something phenomenal in labor statistics. I confess I have felt little enthusiasm for the labor riots which seem epidemic at the North. Carnegie's men at Homestead, for instance, were among the best paid workmen in the country, receiving many of them $240 per month, living luxuriously, dictating their own terms as to who should work with them, how many hours, and what special labor they will perform. Their employers are forced to hire so many and such men—for these laboring despots insist on an exact division of labor, no one must be called on to work outside his specialty. Then they must share profits, but be excused from all concern in losses—a patent adjustable sliding scale for wages which slides up beautifully, but never down! If the Northern laboring man has not become a tyrant, I would like to know what tyranny is.

But I wonder how many know that there are throughout the Southland able bodied, hard working men, toiling year in and year out, from sunrise to dusk, for fifty cents per day, out of which they must feed and shelter and clothe themselves and their families! That they often have to take their wage in tickets convertible into meat, meal and molasses at the village grocery, owned by the same ubiquitous employer! That there are tenants holding leases on farms who toil sixteen hours to the day and work every chick and child in their posession, not sparing even the drudging wife—to find at the end of the harvesting season and the squaring up of accounts that their accumulations have been like gathering water in a sieve.

Do you ask the cause of their persistent poverty? It is not found in the explanation often vouchsafed by the white landlord—that the Negro is indolent, improvident and vicious. Taking them man for man and dollar for dollar, I think you will find the Negro, in ninety-nine cases out of a hundred, not a whit behind the Anglo-Saxon of equal chances. It is a fact which every candid man who rides through the rural districts in the South will admit, that in progressive aspirations and industry the Negro is ahead of the white man of his chances. Indeed it would not be hard to show that the white man *of his chances* does not exist. The "Crackers" and "poor-whites" were never slaves, were never oppressed or discriminated against. Their time, their earnings, their activities have always been at their own disposal; and pauperism in their case can be attributed to nothing but stagnation,—moral, mental, and physical immobility: while in the case of the Negro, poverty can at least be partially accounted for by the hard conditions of life and labor,—the past oppression and continued repression which form the vital air in which the Negro lives and moves and has his being.

One often hears in the North an earnest plea from some lecturer for "our working girls" (of course this means white working girls). And recently I listened to one who went into pious agonies at the thought of the future mothers of Americans having to stand all day at shop counters; and then advertised with applause a philanthropic firm who were giving their girls a trip to Europe for rest and recreation! I am always glad to hear of the establishment of reading rooms and social entertainments to brighten the lot of any women who are toiling for bread—whether they are white women or black women. But how many have ever given a thought to the pinched and down-trodden colored women bending over wash-tubs and ironing boards—with children to feed and house rent to pay, wood to buy, soap and starch to furnish—lugging home weekly great baskets of clothes for families who pay them for a month's laundrying barely enough to purchase a substantial pair of shoes!

Will you call it narrowness and selfishness, then, that I find it impossible to catch the fire of sympathy and enthusiasm for most of these labor movements at the North?

I hear these foreigners, who would boycott an employer if he hired a colored workman, complain of wrong and oppression, of low wages and long hours, clamoring for eight-hour systems and insisting on their right to have sixteen of the twenty-four hours for rest and self-culture, for recreation and social intercourse with families and friends—ah, come with me, I feel like saying, I can show you workingmen's wrong and workingmen's toil which, could it speak, would send up a wail that might be heard from the Potomac to the Rio Grande; and *should it unite and act*, would shake this country from Carolina to California.

But no man careth for their souls. The labor interests of the colored man in this country are as yet dumb and limp. The unorganized mass has found neither tongue nor nerve. In the free and liberal North, thanks to the amalgamated associations and labor unions of immigrant laborers, who cannot even speak English,—the colored man is relegated to the occupations of waiter and barber, unless he has a taste for school teaching or politics. A body of men who still need an interpreter to communicate with their employer, will threaten to cut the nerve and paralyze the progress of an industry that gives work to an American-born citizen, or one which takes measures to instruct any apprentice not supported by the labor monopoly. A skilled mechanic, a friend of mine, secured a job in one of our cities and was seen by union men at work on his house. He was immediately ordered in murderous English to take down his scaffolding and leave the town. Refusing to do so, before night he was attacked by a force that overwhelmed him and he was obliged to leave. Such crushing opposition is not alone against colored persons. These amalgamated and other unions hold and are determined to continue holding an impenetrable monopoly on the labor market, assuming supreme censorship as regards the knowledge and practice of their trade.

In the South, on the other hand, where the colored man virtually holds the labor market, he is too uncertain and unorganized to demand anything like a fair share of the products of his toil. And yet the man who thinks, must see that our labor interests lie at the foundation of our material prosperity. The growth of the colored man in this country must for a long time yet be estimated on his value and productiveness as a laborer. In adding up the account the aggregate of the great toiling mass largely overbalances the few who have acquired means and leisure. The nation judges us as working-men, and poor indeed is that man or race of men who are compelled to toil all the weary years ministering to no higher want than that of bread. To feed is not the chief function of this material that has fallen to our care to be developed and perfected. It is an enormous waste of values to harness the whole man in the narrow furrow, plowing for bread. There are other hungerings in man besides the eternal all-subduing hungering of his despotic stomach. There is the hunger of the eye for beauty, the hunger of the ear for concords, the hun-gering of the mind for development and growth, of the soul for communion and love, for a higher, richer, fuller living—a more abundant life! And every man owes it to himself to *let nothing in him starve* for lack of the proper food. "What is man," says Shakespeare, "if his chief good and market of his time be but to sleep and feed!" Yet such slavery as that is the settled lot of four-fifths the laboring men of the Southland. This, I contend, is an enormous, a profligate waste of the richest possibilities and the divinest aptitudes. And we owe it to humanity, we owe it preeminently to those of our own household, to enlarge and enrich, so far as in us lies, the opportunity and grasp of every soul we can emancipate. Surely there is no greater boon we can bestow on our fellow-man in this life, none that could more truly command his deepest gratitude and love, than to disclose to his soul its possibilities and mend its opportunities,—to place its rootlets in the generous loam, turn its leaves towards the gracious dews and warm sunlight of heaven and let it grow, let it mature in foliage, flower and fruit for GOD AND THE RACE! Philanthropy will devise means—an object is not far to seek.

Closely akin to the value that may be said to have been wasted through the inclemency and barrenness of circumstance, through the sickness, sin and death that wait on poverty and squalor, a large item of worth has undoubtedly been destroyed by mistaken and unscientific manufacture—foolhardy educators rashly attempting to put in some theoretically desirable *crack*—the classical crack, or the professional crack, or the artistic-æsthetic-accomplishments crack— into material better fitted for household pottery and common every-day stone and iron ware. I want nothing I may say to be construed into an attack on classical training or on art development and culture. I believe in allowing every longing of the human soul to attain its utmost reach and grasp. But the effort must be a fizzle which seeks to hammer souls into preconstructed molds and grooves which they have never longed for and cannot be made to take comfort in. The power of appreciation is the measure of an individual's aptitudes; and if a boy hates Greek and Latin and spends all his time whittling out steamboats, it is rather foolish to try to force him into the classics. There may be a locomotive in him, but there is certainly no foreshadowing evidence of either the teacher or preacher. It is a waste of forces to strain his incompetence, and smother his proficiencies. If his hand is far more cunning and clever than his brain, see what he can best do, and give him a chance according to his fitness; try him at a trade.

Industrial training has been hitherto neglected or despised among us, due, I think, as I have said elsewhere, to two causes: first, a mistaken estimate of labor arising from its association with slavery and from its having been despised by the only class in the South thought worthy of imitation; and secondly, the fact that the Negro's ability to work had never been called in question, while his ability to learn Latin and construe Greek syntax needed to be proved to sneering critics. "Scale the heights!" was the cry. "Go to college, study Latin, preach, teach, orate, wear spectacles and a beaver!"

Stung by such imputations as that of Calhoun that if a Negro could prove his ability to master the Greek subjunctive he might vindicate his title to manhood, the newly liberated race first shot forward along this line with an energy and success which astonished its most sanguine friends.

This may not have been most wise. It certainly was quite natural; and the result is we find ourselves in almost as ludicrous a plight as the African in the story, who, after a sermon from his missionary pleading for the habiliments of civilization, complacently donned a Gladstone hat leaving the rest of his body in its primitive simplicity of attire. Like him we began at the wrong end. Wealth must pave the way for learning. Intellect, whether of races or individuals, cannot soar to the consummation of those sublime products which immortalize genius, while the general mind is assaulted and burdened with "what shall we eat, what shall we drink, and wherewithal shall we be clothed." Work must first create wealth, and wealth leisure, before the untrammeled intellect of the Negro, or any other race, can truly vindicate its capabilities. Something has been done intellectually we all know. That one black man has written a Greek grammar is enough to answer Calhoun's sneer; but it is leisure, the natural outgrowth of work and wealth, which must furnish room, opportunity, possibility for the highest endeavor and most brilliant achievement. Labor must be the solid foundation stone—the *sine qua non* of our material value; and the only effective preparation for success in this, as it seems to me, lies in the establishment of industrial and technical schools for teaching our colored youth trades. This necessity is obvious for several reasons. First, a colored child, in most cases, can secure a trade in no other way. We had master mechanics while the Negro was a chattel, and the ingenuity of brain and hand served to enrich the coffers of his owner. But to-day skilled labor is steadily drifting into the hands of white workmen—mostly foreigners. Here it is cornered. The white engineer holds a tight monopoly both of the labor market and of the science of his craft. Nothing would induce him to take a colored apprentice or even to work beside a colored workman. Unless the trades are to fall among the lost arts for us as a people, they must be engrafted on those benevolent institutions for Negro training established throughout the land. The youth must be taught to use his trigonometry in surveying his own and his neighbor's farm; to employ his geology and chemistry in finding out the nature of the soil, the constituents drafted from it by each year's crop and the best way to meet the demand by the use of suitable renewers; to apply his mechanics and physics to the construction and handling of machinery—to the intelligent management of iron works and water works and steam works and electric works. One mind in a family or in a town may show a penchant for art, for literature, for the learned professions, or more bookish lore. You will know it when it is there. No need to probe for it. It is a light that cannot be hid under a bushel—and I would try to enable that mind to go the full length of its desires. Let it follow its bent and develop its talent as far as possible: and the whole community might well be glad to contribute its labor and money for the sustenance and cultivation of this brain. Just as earth gives its raw material, its carbons, hydrogen, and oxygen, for the tree which is to elaborate them into foliage, flower and fruit, so the baser elements, bread and money furnished the true brain worker come back to us with compound interest in the rich thought, the invention, the poem, the painting, the statue. Only let us recognize our assignment and not squander our portion in over fond experiments. James Russell Lowell says, "As we cannot make a silk purse out of a sow's ear, no more can we perform the opposite experiment without having a fine lot of spoiled silk on our hands."

With most of us, however, the material, such as it is, has been already delivered. The working of it up is also well under way. The gold, the silver, the wood, the hay, the stubble, whatever there was at hand has all gone in. Now can the world use it? Is there a demand for it, does it perform the functions for which it was made, and is its usefulness greater than the cost of its production? Does it pay expenses and have anything over.

The world in putting these crucial questions to men and women, or to races and nations, classifies them under two heads—as consumers or producers. The man who consumes as much as he produces is simply *nil*. It is no matter to the world economically speaking whether he is in it or out of it. He is merely one more to count in taking the census. The man who consumes more than he produces is a destroyer of the world's wealth and should be estimated precisely as the housekeeper estimates moths and mice. These are the world's parasites, the shirks, the lazy lubbers who hang around rum shops and enter into mutual relationships with lamp posts to bear each the other's burdens, moralizing all the while (wondrous moralists and orators they often are!) and insisting that the world owes them a living! To be sure the world owes them nothing of the kind. The world would consider it a happy riddance from bad rubbish if they would pay up their debt and move over to Mars. Every day they live their unproductive bodies sink and destroy a regular portion of the world's values. At the very lowest estimate, a boy who has reached the age of twenty, has already burned up between three and four thousand dollars of the world's possessions. This is on the very closest and most economical count; I charge him nothing for fuel or lights, allowing him to have warmed by fires that would have burned for others and estimating the cost simply of what he has eaten and worn, *i. e.* the amount which he has actually sunk of the world's wealth. I put his board at the moderate sum of ten dollars per month, and charge him the phenomenally small amount of thirty dollars a year for clothing and incidentals. This in twenty years gives him a debt of three thousand dollars, which no honest man should be willing to leave the world without settling. The world does not owe them a living then—the world only waits for them to square up and change their residence. It is only they who produce more than they consume, that the world owes, or even acknowledges as having any practical value.

Now to which class do we belong? The question must in the first place be an individual one for every man of whatever race: Am I giving to the world an equivalent of what it has given and is giving me? Have I a margin on the outside of consumption for surplus production? We owe it to the world to give out at least as much as we have taken in, but if we aim to be accounted a positive value we must leave it a little richer than we found it. The boy who dies at twenty leaving three thousand dollars in bank to help another, has just paid expenses. If he lives longer it increases his debit and should be balanced by a corresponding increase on the credit side. The life that serves to develop another, the mother who toils to educate her boy, the father who invests his stored-up capital in education, giving to the world the energies and usefulness of his children trained into a well disciplined manhood and womanhood has paid his debt in the very richest coin,—a coin which is always legal tender, a priceless gift, the most precious payment we can make for what we have received. And we may be sure, if we can give no more than a symmetric life, an inspiring thought, a spark caught from a noble endeavor, its value will not be lost.

Previous to 1793 America was able to produce unlimited quantities of cotton, but unable to free the fibre from the seeds. Eli Whitney came to the rescue of the strangled industry and perfected a machine which did the work needed. The deliverance which he wrought was complete. The following year America's exports of cotton to England were increased from not one pound in previous years to 1,600,000 pounds. He gave dollars.

Just before the battle of Quebec Wolf repeated and enjoyed Gray's Elegy saying he valued that gem more highly than the capture of the city before which he was encamped. The next day the city was taken and Wolf was laid to rest. But the world is in debt to both the poet and the soldier—a boundless debt, to the one for an eternal thought-gem, to the other for immortal heroism and devoted patriotism.

Once there lived among men One whom sorrowing millions for centuries since have joyed to call friend—One whose "come unto me ye that are heavy laden" has given solace and comfort to myriads of the human race. *He gave a life.*

We must as individuals compare our cost with what we are able to give. The worth of a race or a nation can be but the aggregate worth of its men and women. While we need not indulge in offensive boasting, it may not be out of place in a land where there is some adverse criticism and not a little unreasonable prejudice, quietly to take account of stock and see if we really represent a value in this great American commonwealth. The average American is never too prejudiced, I think, to have a keen appreciation for the utilities; and he is certainly not behind the rest of the world in his clear perception of the purchasing power of a dollar. Beginning here, then, I find that, exclusive of the billions of wealth *given* by them to enrich another race prior to the passage of the Thirteenth Amendment, the colored people of America to-day hold in their own right $264,000,000 of taxable property; and this is over and above the $50,000,000 which collapsed in the Freedman's Savings Bank when that gigantic iniquity paralyzed the hope and shocked the faith of an inexperienced and unfinancial people.

One would like to be able to give reliable statistics of the agricultural and mechanical products of the colored laborer, but so far I have not been able to obtain them. It is a modest estimate, I am sure, to ascribe fully two-thirds of the 6,940,000 bales of cotton produced in 1888 to Negro cultivation. The reports give estimates only in bulk as to the products of a state or county. Our efficient and capable census enumerators never draw the color line on labor products. You have no trouble in turning to the page that shows exactly what percentage of colored people are illiterate, or just how many have been condemned by the courts; no use taking the trouble to specify whether it was for the larceny of a ginger cake, or for robbing a bank of a cool half million and skipping off to Canada: it's all crime of course, and crime statistics and illiteracy statistics must be accurately detailed—and colored.

Similar commendable handling meets the colored producer from the managers of our Big American Show at Chicago which we are all so nervously anxious shall put the best foot foremost in bowing to the crowned heads and the gracious lords and ladies from over the waters. To allow any invention or mechanism, art or farm product to be accredited a black man would be drawing the color line! And our immaculate American could never be guilty of anything so vile as drawing a color line!!!

I am unable to say accurately, then, just how many bales of cotton, pounds of tobacco, barrels of molasses and bushels of corn and wheat are given to the world through Negro industry. The same difficulty is met in securing authentic information concerning their inventions and patents. The records of the Patent Office at Washington do not show whether a patentee is white or colored. And all inventions and original suggestions made by a colored man before emancipation were necessarily accredited to some white individual, a slave not being able to take the oath administered to the applicant for a patent. Prof. Wright, however, by simply collecting through personal inquiry the number of colored patentees which could be remembered and identified by examiners and attorneys practicing before the Patent Office authorities, published upwards of fifty in the A. M. E. Review for April, 1886. Doubtless this number was far within the truth, and many new patents have been taken out since his count was made. Almost daily in my walk I pass an ordinary looking black man, who, I am told, is considering an offer of $30,000 for his patent rights on a corn planter, which, by the way, has been chosen as part of the Ohio exhibit for the Columbian Exposition. He has secured as many as half a dozen patents within a few years and is carrying around a "new machine" in his head every day.

Granville Wood, of Cincinnati, has given valuable returns to the world as an electrician; and there is no estimating the money in the outright gift of this people through unremunerated toil. The Negro does not always show a margin over and above consumption; but this does not necessarily in his case prove that he is not a producer. During the agitations for adverse legislation against the Chinese, the charge was alleged that they spent nothing in the country. They hoarded their earnings, lived on nothing, and finally returned to China to live in luxury and to circulate the wealth amassed in this country. A similar complaint can never be lodged against the Negro. Poor fellow, he generally lives pretty well up to his income. He labors for little and spends it all. He has never yet gained the full consent of his mind to "take his gruel a little thinner" till his little pile has grown a bit. He does not like to seem short. And had he the wage of a thousand a year his bigheartedness would immediately put him under the painful necessity of having it do the entertainment of five thousand. He must eat, and is miserable if he can't dress; and seems on the whole internally fitted every way to the style and pattern of a millionaire, rather than to the plain, plodding, stingy old path of common sense and economy. This is a flaw in the *material* of the creature. The grain just naturally runs that way. If our basal question of economics were put to him: "*What do you give—are you adding something every year to the world's stored up capital?*" His ingenuous answer would be, as the ghost of a smile flits across his mobile lips—"Yea, Lord; I give back *all*. I am even now living on the prospects of next year's income. I give my labor at accommodation rates, and forthwith reconvert my wages into the general circulation. Funds, somehow, don't seem to stick to me. I have no talents, or smaller coins either, hid in a napkin." It will be well for him to learn, however, that it is not what we make but what we save that constitutes wealth. The hod-carrier who toils for $1.50 a day, spending the dollar and laying up the half, is richer than the congressman with an annual income of $5000 and annual duns of $8000. What he most urgently needs to learn is systematic saving. He works hard enough generally—but does not seem able to retrench expenses—to cut off the luxuries which people of greater income and larger foresight, seeing to be costly and unnecessary would deny themselves. He wants to set to work vigorously to widen the margin outside the expenditures. He cannot be too deeply impressed with the fact that tobacco and liquors—even leaving out their moral aspects—are too costly to be indulged in by any who are not living on the interest of capital ready in store. A man living on his earnings should eschew luxuries, if he wishes to produce wealth. But when those luxuries deteriorate manhood, they impoverish and destroy the most precious commodity we can offer the world.

For after all, the highest gifts are not measurable in dollars and cents. Beyond and above the class who run an account with the world and merely manage honestly to pay *in kind* for what they receive, there is a noble army—the Shakespeares and Miltons, the Newtons, Galileos and Darwins,—Watts, Morse, Howe, Lincoln, Garrison, John Brown—a part of the world's roll of honor—whose price of board and keep dwindles into nothingness when compared with what the world owes them; men who have taken of the world's bread and paid for it in immortal thoughts, invaluable inventions, new facilities, heroic deeds of loving self-sacrifice; men who dignify the world for their having lived in it and to whom the world will ever bow in grateful worship as its heroes and benefactors. It may not be ours to stamp our genius in enduring characters—but we can give what we are *at its best*.

Visiting the slave market in Boston one day in 1761, Mrs. John Wheatley was attracted by the modest demeanor and intelligent countenance of a delicate looking black girl just from the slave ship. She was quite nude save for a piece of coarse carpet she had tied about her loins, and the only picture she could give of her native home was that she remembered her mother in the early morning every day pouring out water before the rising sun. The benevolent Mrs. Wheatley expended some labor in polishing up this crude gem, and in 1773 the gifted Phillis gave to the world a small octavo volume of one hundred and twenty precious pages, published in London and dedicated to the Countess of Huntingdon. In 1776, for some lines she had sent him, she received from the greatest American the following tribute dated at Cambridge:

> MISS PHILLIS:— . . . I thank you most sincerely for your polite notice of me in the elegant lines you enclosed; and however undeserving I may be of such encomium and panegyric, the style and manner exhibit a striking proof of your poetical talents; in honor of which and as a tribute justly due to you, I would have published the poem had I not been apprehensive that, while I only meant to give the world this new instance of your genius, I might have incurred the imputation of vanity. This and nothing else determined me not to give it place in the public prints. If you should ever come to Cambridge or near headquarters, I shall be happy to see a person so favored by the Muses, and to whom nature has been so liberal and beneficent in her dispensations. I am, with great respect,
>
> Your obedient humble servant,
> GEORGE WASHINGTON.

That girl paid her debts *in song*.

In South Carolina there are two brothers, colored men, who own and conduct one of the most extensive and successful farms in this country for floriculture. Their system of irrigating and fertilizing is the most scientific in the state, and by their original and improved methods of grafting and cultivating they have produced a new and rich variety of the rose called *Loiseaux*, from their name. Their roses are famous throughout Europe and are specially prized by the French for striking and marvellous beauty. The Loiseaux brothers send out the incense of their grateful returns to the world in the *sweet fragrance of roses*.

Some years ago a poor and lowly orphan girl stood with strange emotions before a statue of Benjamin Franklin in Boston. Her bosom heaved and her eyes filled as she whispered between her clenched teeth, "Oh, how I would like to make a stone man?" Wm. Lloyd Garrison became her providence and enlarged her opportunity; *she paid for it* in giving to the world the *Madonna with the Christ and adoring Angels*, now in the collection of the Marquis of Bute. From her studio in Rome Edmonia Lewis, the colored sculptress, continues to increase the debt of the world to her by her graceful thoughts in the chaste marble.

On May 27, 1863, a mixed body of troops in blue stood eagerly expectant before a rebel stronghold. On the extreme right of the line, a post of honor and of danger, were stationed the Negro troops, the first and third regiments of the Louisiana Native Guards. On going into action, says an eye witness, they were 1080 strong, and formed into four lines, Lieut.-Colonel Bassett, 1st Louisiana, forming the first line, and Lieut.-Colonel Henry Finnegas the second. Before any impression had been made upon the earth works of the enemy, and in full face of the batteries belching forth their sixty-two pounders, the order to charge was given,—and the black regiment rushed forward to encounter grape, canister, shell and musketry, having no artillery but two small howitzers—which seemed mere pop-guns to their adversaries—and with no reserve whatever. The terrible fire from the rebel guns upon the unprotected masses mowed them down like grass. Colonel Bassett being driven back, Colonel Finnegas took his place, and his men being similarly cut to pieces, Bassett reformed and recommenced. And thus these brave fellows went on from 7 o'clock in the morning till 3:30 p. m., under the most hideous carnage that men ever had to withstand. During this time they rallied and were ordered to make six distinct charges, losing thirty-seven killed, one hundred and fifty-five wounded, and one hundred and sixteen missing, "the majority, if not all of these," adds a correspondent of the New York Times, who was an eye witness of the fight, "being in all probability now lying dead on the gory field without the rights of sepulture! *for when, by flag of truce our forces in other directions were permitted to reclaim their dead, the benefit, through some neglect, was not extended to these black regiments.*"

"The deeds of heroism," he continues, "performed by these colored men were such as the proudest white men might emulate. Their colors are torn to pieces by shot, and literally bespattered by blood and brains. The color-sergeant of the 1st La. on being mortally wounded, hugged the colors to his breast when a struggle ensued between the two color-corporals on each side of him as to who should bear the sacred standard—and during this generous contention one of the corporals was wounded. One black lieutenant mounted the enemy's works three or four times, and in one charge the assaulting party came within fifty paces of them. If only ordinarily supported by artillery and reserve, no one can convince us that they would not have opened a passage through the enemy's works. Captain Callioux, of the 1st La., a man so black that he prided himself on his blackness, died the death of a hero leading on his men in the thickest of the fight. One poor wounded fellow came along with his arm shattered by a shell, jauntily swinging it with the other, as he said to a friend of mine: 'Massa, guess I can fight no more.' I was with one of the captains looking after the wounded, when we met one limping along toward the front. Being asked where he was going, he said, 'I been shot in de leg, cap'n, an' dey wants me to go to de hospital—hut I reckon I c'n gib 'em some mo' yit.'"

Says Major-General Banks in the report from Headquarters of the Army of the Gulf, before Port Hudson, May 30, 1863, writing to Major-General Halleck, General-in-Chief at Washington: "The position occupied by the Negro troops was one of importance and called for the utmost steadiness and bravery in those to whom it was confided. It gives me pleasure to report that they answered every expectation. Their conduct was heroic. No troops could be more determined or more daring."

> "'Charge!' Trump and drum awoke,
> Onward the bondmen broke;
> Bayonet and sabre-stroke
> Vainly opposed their rush.
> Through the wild battle's crush,
> With but one thought aflush,
> Driving their lords like chaff,
> In the guns' mouths they laugh;
> Or at the slippery brands

Leaping with open hands,
Down they bear man and horse,
Down in their awful course;
Trampling with bloody heel
Over the crashing steel,
All their eyes forward bent,
Rushed the black regiment.

'Freedom!' their battle-cry—
'Freedom! or leave to die!'
Ah! and they meant the word,
Not as with us 'tis heard,
Not a mere party-shout:
They gave their spirits out.
Trusted the end to God,
And on the gory sod
Rolled in triumphant blood!"

And thus they paid *their debt.* "They gave—*their spirits out!*"

In the heart of what is known as the "Black Belt" of Alabama and within easy reach of the great cotton plantations of Georgia, Mississippi, and Florida, a devoted young colored man ten years ago started a school with about thirty Negro children assembled in a comical looking shanty at Tuskegee. His devotion was contagious and his work grew; an abandoned farm of 100 acres was secured and that gradually grew to 640 acres, largely wood-land, on which a busy and prosperous school is located; and besides a supply farm was added, of heavy rich land, 800 acres, from which grain and sugar cane are main products. Since 1881, 2,947 students have been taught here, of whom 102 have graduated, while 200 more have received enough training to fit them to do good work as teachers, intelligent farmers, and mechanics. The latest enrollment shows girls, 247; boys, 264. Of the 102 graduates, 70 per cent. are teachers, ministers and farmers. They usually combine teaching and farming. Three are printers (learned the trades at school), one is a tinner, one a blacksmith, one a wheel-wright, three are merchants, three are carpenters, others in the professions or filling miscellaneous positions.

That man is paying his debt by giving to this country *living, working, consecrated men and women!*

Now each can give something. It may not be a poem, or marble bust, or fragrant flower even; it may not be ours to place our lives on the altar of country as a loving sacrifice, or even to devote our living activities so extensively as B. T. Washington to supplying the world's need for strong and willing helpers. But we can at least *give ourselves*. Each can be *one* of those strong willing helpers—even though nature has denied him the talent of endlessly multiplying his force. And nothing less can honorably cancel our debt. Each is under a most sacred obligation not to squander the material committed to him, not to sap its strength in folly and vice, and to see at the least that he delivers a product worthy the labor and cost which have been expended on him. A sound manhood, a true womanhood is a fruit which the lowliest can grow. And it is a commodity of which the supply never exceeds the demand. There is no danger of the market being glutted. The world will always want *men*. The worth of one is infinite. To this value all other values are merely relative. Our money, our schools, our governments, our free institutions, our systems of religion and forms of creeds are all first and last to be judged by this standard: what sort of men and women do they grow? How are men and women being shaped and molded by this system of training, under this or that form of government, by this or that standard of moral action? You propose a new theory of education; *what sort of men does it turn out?* Does your system make boys and girls superficial and mechanical? Is it a producing of average percentages or a rounding out of manhood,—a sound, thorough, and practical development,—or a scramble for standing and marks?

We have a notion here in America that our political institutions,—the possibilities of a liberal and progressive democracy, founded on universal suffrage and in some hoped-for, providential way *compelling* universal education and devotion,—our peculiar American attainments are richly worth all they have cost in blood and anguish. But our form of government, divinely ordered as we dream it to be, must be brought to the bar to be tested by this standard. It is nothing worth of itself—independently of whether it furnishes a good atmosphere in which to cultivate men. Is it developing a self respecting freedom, a sound manliness on the part of *the individual*—or does it put into the power of the wealthy few the opportunity and the temptation to corrupt the many? If our vaunted "*rule of the people*" does not breed nobler men and women than monarchies have done—it must and will inevitably give place to something better.

I care not for the theoretical symmetry and impregnable logic of your moral code, I care not for the hoary respectability and traditional mysticisms of your theological institutions, I care not for the beauty and solemnity of your rituals and religious ceremonies, I care not even for the reasonableness and unimpeachable fairness of your social ethics,—if it does not turn out better, nobler, truer men and women,—if it does not add to the world's stock of valuable souls,—if it does not give us a sounder, healthier, more reliable product from this great factory of *men*—I will have none of it. I shall not try to test your logic, but weigh your results—and that test is the *measure of the stature of the fullness of a man*. You need not formulate and establish the credibility and authenticity of Christian Evidences, when you can demonstrate and prove the present value of CHRISTIAN MEN. And this test for systems of belief, for schools of thought, and for theories of conduct, is also the ultimate and inevitable test of nations, of races and of individuals. What sort of men do you turn out? *How* are you supplying the great demands of the world's market? What is your true value? This, we may be sure, will be the final test by which the colored man in America will one day be judged in the cool, calm, unimpassioned, unprejudiced second thought of the American people.

Let us then quietly commend ourselves to this higher court—this final tribunal. Short sighted idiosyncracies are but transient phenomena. It is futile to combat them, and unphilosophical to be depressed by them. To allow such things to overwhelm us, or even to absorb undue thought, is an admission of weakness. As sure as time *is*—*these mists will clear away*. And the world—our world, will surely and unerringly see us as we are. Our only care need be the intrinsic worth of our contributions. If we represent the ignorance and poverty, the vice and destructiveness, the vagabondism and parasitism in the world's economy, no amount of philanthropy and benevolent sentiment can win for us esteem: and if we contribute a positive value in those things the world prizes, no amount of negrophobia can ultimately prevent its recognition. And our great "problem" after all is to be solved not by brooding over it, and orating about it, but by *living into it*.

THE GAIN FROM A BELIEF

A SOLITARY FIGURE stands in the market-place, watching as from some lonely tower the busy throng that hurry past him. A strange contrast his cold, intellectual eye to the eager, strained, hungry faces that surge by in their never ending quest of wealth, fame, glory, bread.

Mark his pallid cheek and haggard brow, and the fitful gleam of those restless eyes like two lone camp-fires on a deserted plain.

Why does that smile, half cynical, half sad, flit across his countenance as he contemplates these mighty heart-throbs of human passions and woes, human hopes and human fears? Is it pity—is it contempt—is it hate for this struggling, working, believing humanity which curls those lips and settles upon that hitherto indifferent brow?

Who is he?

Earth's skepticism looking on at the protean antics of earth's enthusiasms. Speculative unbelief, curiously and sneeringly watching the humdrum, common-place, bread-and-butter toil of unspeculative belief. Lofty, unimpassioned agnosticism, *that thinks*—face to face with hobbling, blundering, unscientific faith, *that works*.

Dare we approach?

"Sir: I perceive you are not drawn into the whirl-pool of hurrying desires that sweep over earth's restless sons. Your philosophy, I presume, lifts you above the toils and anxieties, the ambitions and aspirations of the common herd. Pardon me, but do you not feel called to devote those superior powers of yours to the uplifting of your less favored brethren? May not you pour the oil of human kindness and love on these troubled waters? May not your wisdom shape and direct the channel of this tortuous stream, building up here, and clearing out there, till this torrent become once more a smiling river, reflecting Heaven's pure love in its silvery bosom, and again this fruitful valley blossom with righteousness and peace? Does not your soul burn within you as you look on this seething

139

mass of struggling, starving, sinning souls? Are you not inspired to
lift up despairing, sinking, grovelling man,—to wipe the grime and
tears from his marred countenance, and bid him Look aloft and be
strong, Repent and be saved, Trust God and live!"

Ah! the coldness of the look he turned on me! Methought
'twould freeze my soul. "Poor fool!" it seemed to say; and yet I
could not but think I discovered a trace of sadness as he replied:—

"What is man?—A curiously fashioned clock; a locomotive,
capable of sensations;—a perfected brute. Man is a plant that grows
and thinks; the form and place of his growth and the product of his
thought are as little dependent on his will or effort as are the bark,
leaves, and fruit of a tree on its choice. Food, soil, climate,—these
make up the man,—the whole man, his life, his soul (if he have
one). Man's so-called moral sense is a mere dance of molecules; his
spiritual nature, a pious invention. Remorse is a blunder, repen-
tance is vain, self-improvement or reformation an impossibility.
The laws of matter determine the laws of intellect, and these shape
man's nature and destiny and are as inevitable and uncontrollable as
are the laws of gravitation and chemical affinity. You would-be
reformers know not the stupendous nonsense you are talking. Man
is as little responsible for vice or crime as for fever or an earthquake.
Those in whom the cerebrum shows a particular formation, will
make their holidays in gambling, betting, drinking, horseracing—
their more serious pursuits in stealing, ravening, murdering. They
are not immoral any more than a tiger is immoral; they are simply
*un*moral. They need to be restrained, probably, as pests of society,
or submitted to treatment as lunatics. Their fellows in whom the
white and gray matter of the brain cells are a little differently cor-
related, will in their merry moods sing psalms and make it their
habitual activity to reach out after the Unknown in various ways,
trying to satisfy the vague and restless longings of what they call
their souls by punishing themselves and pampering the poor. I have
neither blame nor praise. Each class simply believe and do as they
must. And as for God—science finds him not. If there be a God—
He is unknown and unknowable. The finite mind of man cannot
conceive the Infinite and Eternal. And if such a being exists, he
cannot be concerned about the miserable wretches of earth.
Searching after him is vain. Man has simply projected his own personality into space and worshipped it as a God—a person—himself.
My utmost knowledge is limited to a series of sensations within,

aware of itself; and a possibility of sensations without, both governed by unbending laws within the limits of experience and a
reasonable distance beyond."

"And beyond that Beyond" I ask breathlessly—"beyond that
Beyond?"

I am sure I detected just then a tremor as of a chill running
through that fragile frame; and the eye, at first thoughtful and
coldly scornful only, is now unmistakably shaded with sadness.
"Beyond that Beyond?" he repeated slowly,—beyond that Beyond,
if there be such,—*spaces of darkness and eternal silence!*

Whether this prolonged throb of consciousness exist after its
external possibilities have been dissolved—I cannot tell. That is to
me—a horrible plunge—*in the dark!* I stand at the confluence of
two eternities and three immensities. I see, with Pascal, only infin-
ities in all directions which envelop me like an atom—like a
shadow which endures for a moment and—will never return! All
that I know is that I must die, but what I know the very least of is
that very death—which I can not avoid! *The eternal silence* of these
infinite spaces maddens me!"

Sick at heart, I turn away and ask myself what is this system
which, in the words of Richter, makes the universe an automaton,
and man's future—a coffin! Is this the cold region to which
thought, as it moves in its orbit, has brought us in the nineteenth
century? Is this the germ of the "Philosophy of the future"—the
exponent of our "advanced ideas," the "new light" of which our
age so uproariously boasts? Nay rather is not this *monstruum horren-*
dum of our day but a renewal of the empiricism and skepticism of
the days of Voltaire? Here was undoubtedly the nucleus of the
cloud no bigger than a man's hand, which went on increasing in
bulk and blackness till it seemed destined to enshroud earth and
heaven in the gloom of hell.

David Hume, who, though seventeen years younger than
Voltaire, died in 1776 just two years before the great French skeptic,
taught skepticism in England on purely metaphysical grounds.
Hume knew little or nothing about natural science; but held that
what we call mind consists merely of successive perceptions, and
that we can have no knowledge of anything but phenomena. His
system afterwards passes through France, is borrowed and filtered
through the brain of a half crazy French schoolmaster, Auguste
Conte, who thus becomes the founder of the Contist school of

Positivism or Nescience or Agnosticism as it is variously called. The adherents of his school admit neither revelation, nor a God, nor the immortality of the soul. Conte held, among other things, that two hours a day should be spent in the worship of Collective Humanity to be symbolized by some of the *sexe aimant*. On general principles it is not quite clear which is the *sexe aimant*. But as Conte proceeds to mention one's wife, mother, and daughter as fitting objects of religious adoration because they represent the present, past and future of Humanity—one is left to infer that he considered the female the *loving sex* and the ones to be worshipped; though he does not set forth who were to be objects of woman's own adoring worship. In this ecclesiastical system which Prof. Huxley wittily denominates *Romanism minus Christianity*, Conte made himself High Pontiff, and his inamorata, the widow of a galley slave, was chief saint. This man was founder of the system which the agnostic prefers to the teachings of Jesus! However, had this been all, the positivist would have been as harmless as any other lunatic. But he goes a step farther and sets up his system as the philosophy of *natural science*, originating in and proved by pure observation and investigation of physical phenomena; and scoffs at as presumptuous and unwarrantable all facts that cannot be discerned through the senses. In this last position he is followed by John Stuart Mill, Herbert Spencer, G. H. Lewes, and a noble army of physicists, naturalists, physiologists, and geologists. Says one:"We have no knowledge of anything but phenomena, and the essential nature of phenomena and their ultimate causes are unknown and inscrutable to us." Says another: "All phenomena without exception are governed by invariable laws with which no volitions natural or supernatural interfere." And another: "Final causes are unknown to us and the search after them is fruitless, a mere chase of a favorite will-o-the-wisp. We know nothing about any supposed purposes for which organs 'were made.' Birds fly because they have wings, a true naturalist will never say—he can never know they have wings *in order that* they may fly."

And Mr. Ingersoll, the American exponent of positivism, in his "Why I Am an Agnostic," winds up a glittering succession of epigrammatic inconsistencies with these words: "Let us be honest with ourselves. In the presence of countless mysteries, standing beneath the boundless heaven sown thick with constellations, knowing that each grain of sand, each leaf, each blade of grass, asks of every mind the answerless question; knowing that the simplest thing defies solution; feeling that we deal with the superficial and the relative and that we are forever eluded by the real, the absolute,—let us admit the limitations of our minds, and let us have the courage and the candor to say: we do not know."

It is no part of my purpose to enter into argument against the agnostics. Had I the wish, I lack the ability. It is enough for me to know that they have been met by foemen worthy their steel and that they are by no means invincible.

"The average man," says Mr. Ingersoll, "does not reason—he feels." And surely 'twere presumption for an average woman to attempt more. For my part I am content to 'feel.' The brave Switzer who sees the awful avalanche stealing down the mountain side threatening death and destruction to all he holds dear, hardly needs any very correct ratiocination on the mechanical and chemical properties of ice. He *feels* there is danger nigh and there is just time for him to sound the tocsin of alarm and shout to his dear ones 'fly!'

For me it is enough to know that by this system God and Love are shut out; prayer becomes a mummery; the human will but fixed evolutions of law; the precepts and sanctions of morality a lie; the sense of responsibility a disease. The desire for reformation and for propagating conviction is thus a fire consuming its tender. Agnosticism has nothing to impart. Its sermons are the exhortations of one who convinces you he stands on nothing and urges you to stand there too. If your creed is that nothing is sure, there is certainly no spur to proselytize. As in an icicle the agnostic abides alone. The vital principle is taken out of all endeavor for improving himself or bettering his fellows. All hope in the grand possibilities of life are blasted. The inspiration of beginning now a growth which is to mature in endless development through eternity is removed from our efforts at self culture. The sublime conception of life as the seed-time of character for the growing of a congenial inner-self to be forever a constant conscious presence is changed into the base alternative conclusion, *Let us eat and drink for to-morrow we die.*

To my mind the essence of the poison is just here. As far as the metaphysical grounds for skepticism are concerned, they are as harmless to the masses as if they were entombed in Greek or Hebrew. Many of the terms, it is true, are often committed to memory and paraded pretty much in the spirit of the college sophomore who affects gold-bowed spectacles and stooping shoulders—it is scholarly, you know. But the real reasons for and against agnosticism rest on

psychological and scientific facts too abstruse for the laity to appreciate. There is much subtle sophistry in the oracular utterances of a
popular speaker like Mr. Ingersoll, which catch the fancy and charm
the imagination of the many. His brilliant blasphemies like the
winged seed of the thistle are borne on the slightest breath of wind
and find lodgment in the shallowest of soils; while the refutation of
them, undertaken in a serious and logical vein is often too conclusive
to convince: that is, it is too different in kind to reach the same class
of minds that have been inoculated with the poison germs.

My own object, however, is neither to argue nor to refute argument here. I want to utter just this one truth:—The great, the fundamental need of any nation, any race, is for heroism, devotion,
sacrifice; and there cannot be heroism, devotion, or sacrifice in a
primarily skeptical spirit. A great man said of France, when she was
being lacerated with the frantic stripes of her hysterical children,—
France needs a religion! And the need of France during her trying
Revolution is the need of every crisis and conflict in the evolution of
nations and races. At such times most of all, do men need to be
anchored to what they *feel* to be eternal verities. And nothing else at
any time can propel men into those sublime efforts of altruism which
constitute the moral heroes of humanity. The demand for heroism,
devotion and sacrifice founded on such a faith is particularly urgent
in a race at almost the embryonic stage of character-building. The
Hour is *now*,—where is the man? He must *believe* in the infinite possibilities of devoted self-sacrifice and in the eternal grandeur of a
human idea heroically espoused. It is the enthusiasms, the faiths of the
world that have heated the crucibles in which were formed its refor-
mations and its impulses toward a higher growth. And I do not mean
by faith the holding of correct views and unimpeachable opinions on
mooted questions, merely; nor do I understand it to be the ability to
forge cast-iron formulas and dub them TRUTH. For while I do not
deny that absolute and eternal truth *is*,—still truth must be infinite,
and as incapable as infinite space, of being encompassed and confined
by one age or nation, sect or country—much less by one little creature's finite brain.

To me, faith means *treating the truth as true.* Jesus *believed* in the
infinite possibilities of an individual soul. His faith was a triumphant
realization of the eternal development of *the best* in man—an opti-
mistic vision of the human aptitude for endless expansion and

perfectibility. This truth to him placed a sublime valuation on each individual sentiency—a value magnified infinitely by reason of its immortal destiny. He could not lay hold of this truth and let pass an opportunity to lift men into nobler living and firmer building. He could not lay hold of this truth and allow his own benevolence to be narrowed and distorted by the trickeries of circumstance or the colorings of prejudice.

Life must be something more than dilettante speculation. And religion (ought to be if it isn't) a great deal more than mere gratification of the instinct for worship linked with the straight-teaching of irreproachable credos. Religion must be *life made true;* and life is action, growth, development—begun now and ending never. And a life made true cannot confine itself—it must reach out and twine around every pulsing interest within reach of its uplifting tendrils. If then you *believe* that intemperance is a growing vice among a people within touch of your sympathies; if you see that, whereas the "Lord had shut them in," so that from inheritance there are but few cases of alcoholized blood,—yet that there is danger of their becoming under their changed circumstances a generation of inebriates—if you believe this, then this is your truth. Take up your parable and in earnestness and faith *give it out* by precept and by example.

Do you *believe* that the God of history often chooses the weak things of earth to confound the mighty, and that the Negro race in America has a veritable destiny in His eternal purposes,—then don't spend your time discussing the 'Negro Problem' amid the clouds of your fine havanna, ensconced in your friend's well-cushioned armchair and with your patent leather boot-tips elevated to the opposite mantel. Do those poor "cowards in the South" need a leader—then get up and lead them! Let go your purse-strings and begin to *live* your creed. Or is it your modicum of truth that God hath made of one blood all nations of the earth; and that all interests which specialize and contract the broad, liberal, cosmopolitan idea of universal brotherhood and equality are narrow and pernicious, then treat that truth as true. Don't inveigh against lines of longitude drawn by others when at the same time you are applying your genius to devising lines of latitude which are neither race lines, nor character lines, nor intelligence lines—but certain social-appearance circlets assorting your "universal brotherhood" by shapes of noses and texture of hair. If you object to imaginary lines—don't draw them! Leave only the real lines of nature and character. And so whatever the vision, the revelation, the idea, vouchsafed *you*,

Think it truly and thy thoughts shall the soul's famine feed.
Speak it truly and each word of thine shall be a fruitful seed;
Live it truly and thy life shall be a grand and holy creed!

Macaulay has left us in his masterly description of Ignatius Loyola a vivid picture of the power of a belief and its independence of material surroundings.

'On the road from the Theatine convent in Venice might have been seen once a poor crippled Spaniard, wearily but as fast as his injured limbs can carry him making his way toward Rome. His face is pinched, his body shrunken, from long fast and vigil. He enters the City of the Cæsars without money, without patrons, without influence! but there burns a light in his eye that recks not of despair. In a frequented portion of a busy street he stops and mounts a stone, and from this rude rostrum begins to address the passers by in barbarous Latin. Lo, there is contagion in the man! He has actually imparted of his spirit to that mottled audience! And now the same fire burns in a hundred eyes, that shone erewhile from his. Men become his willing slaves to do his bidding even unto the ends of the earth. With what courage, what zeal, what utter self-abnegation, with what blind devotion to their ends regardless of means do they preach, teach, write, act! Behind the thrones of kings, at the bedside of paupers, under every disguise in every land, mid pestilence and famine, in prisons oft, in perils by land and perils by sea, the Jesuit, undaunted, pursues his way.'

Do you seek to know the secret charm of Ignatius Loyola, the hidden spring of the Jesuit's courage and unfaltering purpose? It is these magic words, "*I believe*." That is power. That is the stamping attribute in every impressive personality, that is the fire to the engine and the moter force in every battery. That is the live coal from the altar which at once unseals the lips of the dumb—and that alone which makes a man a positive and not a negative quantity in the world's arithmetic. With this potent talisman man no longer "abideth alone." He cannot stand apart, a cold spectator of earth's pulsing struggles. The flame must burst forth. The idea, the doctrine, the device for betterment must be imparted. "*I believe*,"—this was strength and power to Paul, to Mohammed, to the Saxon

Monk and the Spanish Zealot,—and they must be our strength if our lives are to be worth the living. They mean as much today as they did in the breast of Luther or of Loyola. Who cheats me of this robs me of both shield and spear. Without them I have no inspiration to better myself, no inclination to help another.

It is small service to humanity, it seems to me, to open men's eyes to the fact that the world rests on nothing. Better the turtle of the myths, than a *perhaps*. If "fooled they must he, though wisest of the wise," let us help to make them the fools of virtue. You may have learned that the pole star is twelve degrees from the pole and forbear to direct your course by it—preferring your needle taken from earth and fashioned by man's device. The slave brother, however, from the land of oppression once saw the celestial beacon and dreamed not that it ever deviated from due North. He *believed* that *somewhere* under its beckoning light, lay a far away country where a man's a man. He sets out with his heavenly guide before his face— would you tell him he is pursuing a wandering light? Is he the poorer for his ignorant hope? Are you the richer for your enlightened suspicion?

Yes, I believe there is existence beyond our present experience; that that existence is conscious and culturable; and that there is a noble work here and now in helping men to live *into* it.

> "Not in Utopia,—subterraneous fields,—
>   Or some secreted island, Heaven knows where!
>   But in this very world, which is the world
>   Of all of us—the place where in the end
>   We find our happiness, or not at all!"

There are nations still in darkness to whom we owe a light. The world is to be moved one generation forward—whether by us, by blind force, by fate, or by God! If thou believest, all things are possible; and *as* thou believest, so be it unto thee.

FINIS.